T0244485

PRAISE FOR *THE SKILL CODE*

"If you're worried about your skills becoming obsolete, this book may be your saving grace. Matt Beane has spent his career studying how to gain and maintain expertise as technology evolves, and his analysis is both engrossing and edifying."

—Adam Grant, number one *New York Times* bestselling author of *Hidden Potential* and *Think Again*, and host of the TED podcast *WorkLife*

"Beane shows us the true human-centered approach to AI advancements and how we must act now to achieve the next generation of human skills coupled with the productivity gains from AI."

—Fei-Fei Li, Sequoia Professor of Computer Science and founding director of the Stanford Institute for Human-Centered Artificial Intelligence (HAI) at Stanford University

"AI is unlocking stunning new advances for society. Matt Beane has spent years meticulously researching the fundamentals of how humans learn, develop, and pass on skill in that modern landscape. In *The Skill Code*, Beane delivers an essential road map for how we can combine the best of intelligent technologies with the insights from thousands of years of expert-novice training to reach the brightest possible future."

—Reid Hoffman, cofounder of Inflection AI and LinkedIn, and partner at Greylock

"In his delightful exploration of how people acquire skills for work, Matt Beane integrates wide-ranging research on how we become proficient with the revelation of some hidden challenges to skill development stemming from AI. With riveting stories, *The Skill Code* offers a timeless recipe—challenge, complexity, and connection—for learning and thriving at work."

—Amy Edmondson, Novartis Professor of Leadership and
Management at the Harvard Business School and author
of *Right Kind of Wrong: The Science of Failing Well*

"Matt's decades-long curiosity about human work positions him perfectly to offer such a thoughtful and well-researched guide to skill development in this age of generative AI. *The Skill Code* is a wake-up call for organizations of all sizes."

—Jeff Wilke, former CEO of Amazon Worldwide
Consumer and chairman of Re:Build Manufacturing

"With work changing faster than ever before due to new technology, there has never been a more important time for a book like *The Skill Code*, or anyone more qualified to tell us what it all means than Matt Beane. Here you will find the keys to understanding expertise, by one of the hottest researchers in the field, written in a way that is both readable and actionable and full of the latest research. It's urgent that we learn the lessons in *The Skill Code*."

—Ethan Mollick, professor at the Wharton School
of the University of Pennsylvania and author of
Co-Intelligence: Living and Working with AI

"In *The Skill Code*, Matt Beane explains how challenge, complexity, and connection can and must be combined in our rapidly changing workplace. With academic rigor and actionable insights, this watershed work offers a new approach to skill development that aligns the rigor of traditional apprenticeship with the innovative potential of intelligent tools. A must-read for the architects of tomorrow's workforce."

—Erik Brynjolfsson, director of the Stanford Digital
Economy Lab and coauthor of *The Second Machine Age*

"As machines can do more and more, many are worried that we'll need people less and less. In this vital book, Beane focuses us on a much more immediate and real concern: that powerful technologies give people fewer opportunities to *learn* as they try to master a difficult craft. The ancient human practice of apprenticeship is in trouble; if we want to salvage it, we'd better listen to him."

—Andrew McAfee, author of *The Geek Way*
and coauthor of *The Second Machine Age*

"As a proponent of computer science education, I believe this book is a must-read for anyone looking to understand the critical role of mentorship and hands-on learning in mastering not only technology but any skill. Beane's exploration of the expert-novice dynamic and its evolution in the face of advancing technologies offers invaluable lessons for educators, learners, and leaders alike. This book is a compelling reminder of the timeless importance of human guidance in an increasingly automated world."

—Hadi Partovi, founder and CEO of Code.org

"Matt Beane's *The Skill Code* is a rollicking read; it's magnificently researched and, above all, a relentlessly useful and timely playbook. It shows how to build workplaces where each new generation of experts practice their craft better than the last, have more challenging and better paying jobs, and have stronger bonds with novices than ever before. Along the way, Beane shows what leaders, experts, and novices can do to build organizations that bring out the best in our human abilities, and our zest for life, by harnessing (rather than being replaced or controlled by) the onslaught of new technologies—especially artificial intelligence tools."

—Robert I. Sutton, professor at Stanford University and
New York Times bestselling author or coauthor of *Good Boss,
Bad Boss; Scaling Up Excellence;* and *The Friction Project*

THE **SKILL**
CODE

THE SKILL CODE

HOW TO SAVE
HUMAN ABILITY IN
AN AGE OF
INTELLIGENT MACHINES

MATT BEANE

HARPER
BUSINESS
An Imprint of HarperCollins*Publishers*

HarperCollins books may be purchased for educational, business, or sales promotional use. For information, please email the Special Markets Department at SPsales@harpercollins.com.

FIRST EDITION

Library of Congress Cataloging-in-Publication Data
Names: Beane, Matthew I. (Matthew Ian), author.
Title: The skill code : how to save human ability in an age of intelligent machines / Matt Beane.
Description: First edition. | New York, NY : HarperBusiness, [2024] | Includes bibliographical references and index.
Identifiers: LCCN 2023052328 (print) | LCCN 2023052329 (ebook) | ISBN 9780063337794 (hardcover) | ISBN 9780063337800 (ebook)
Subjects: LCSH: Labor supply—Effect of automation on. | Employees—Effect of automation on. | Skilled labor. | Automation—Economic aspects.
Classification: LCC HD6331 .B43 2024 (print) | LCC HD6331 (ebook) | DDC 331.25—dc23/eng/20231130
LC record available at https://lccn.loc.gov/2023052328
LC ebook record available at https://lccn.loc.gov/2023052329

24 25 26 27 28 LBC 5 4 3 2 1

TO KRISTEN

With all due respect to my former professors, I've long believed I gained more knowledge in kitchens, bars, and dining rooms than any college could even hold.

—ANTHONY BOURDAIN

CONTENTS

CONTENTS

THE SKILL
CODE

CHAPTER ONE

THE SKILL CODE

On a crisp October day when I was nine, with my chin on a splintery fence post, I watched a master tinsmith work with his apprentice to transform a sheet of tin into a candleholder. On every field trip to colonial Old Sturbridge Village in central Massachusetts, that relationship was the main event.

The candleholder was interesting—together they shaped a useful tool from raw materials—but I was transfixed by the way the expert shaped the *apprentice*. Just as the expert kept the tin warm to be pliable, so he kept the apprentice challenged, pushed them to engage with more and more of the crafting process, and depended on them in a way that built a firm, trusting connection. Not much talk, by the way. Gestures, nodding, and head shaking. The expert taking over for advanced technique—holding the piece just so, with the apprentice watching like a hawk. The laughter they shared when something went a bit screwy with the tin.

My whole life I've been fascinated by this special human relationship. Watching mechanics in the shop while we waited for an oil change. Listening to carpenters at home construction sites as they framed up a house. Hearing stories about clinical supervision as my wife went through her training as a therapist. Scene by scene, role by role, year by year, to me this relationship always felt elemental—part of what makes us human. But it was only in graduate school that I deeply digested eighty years of research that pointed to one, clear conclusion: this special working bond between experts and learners has been the bedrock of humanity's transfer of skills and ingenuity for millennia. Many, many millennia.

THE 160,000-YEAR-OLD SCHOOL, HIDDEN IN PLAIN SIGHT

Consider ancient Athens, 507 BC. Twelve-year-old Menelaos begins his second year as apprentice to Stephanos, the master sculptor. Today, like yesterday, he walks to the carpenter's workshop for lumber. Then to the brass smith for pins and braces. Brings it all back and keeps it organized as the senior boys finish the scaffolding for a new piece. All day, he hauls blocks of marble around the workshop, directed by the senior boys, who take their cues from Stephanos. As the sun goes down, he's cleaning up after everyone. Throughout, he's been watching. Noticing the marble scraps and bent tools. Listening as they told stories and talked technique. Asking a question or two while he did his work. Next year, if he works hard, he'll be splitting the marble. Keeping tools organized and sharp. And learning about the next tasks up the apprenticeship chain—roughing out blocks, negotiating for supplies, talking to customers. And six years later, he will be carving his first solo work in his own studio on the outskirts of the city, new apprentices looking up to him. This is all likely true, by the way: we have one of his masterworks, a marble statue of Orestes and Electra, signed "Menelaos, the pupil of Stephanos."[1]

Fast-forward to Rochester, Minnesota, 2020. It's 6:30 in the morning when twenty-six-year-old Kristen wheels her prostate patient into the operating room. She's a resident, a surgeon in training—it's her job to learn. Today she's hoping to do some nerve-sparing—a precise kind of dissection that can preserve erectile function. This is one of surgery's most delicate techniques, and it's critical to the success of the procedure. Kristen and the team put the patient under anesthesia, and she leads the initial eight-inch incision in the lower abdomen. Once she's got the skin, fascia, and muscle clamped back, she tells the nurse to call the attending surgeon. He arrives, gowns up, and for the rest of the two-hour surgery their four hands are mostly inside the patient's body, with Kristen leading the way under the attending surgeon's watchful guidance. When the prostate is out—and, yes, the surgeon let Kristen do a little nerve-sparing—he rips off his scrubs. He starts to do paperwork. Kristen closes the patient by 8:15, with a junior resident looking over her shoulder. She even lets him do the final line of sutures. There's about half an hour of the procedure to go, but Kristen feels great. The patient is going to be fine, and no doubt she's a better surgeon than she was at 6:30.

Think about your most valuable skill. The thing you can reliably do under pressure that delivers results—and looks like magic to those nearby. How did you learn it? Decades of research suggest that you achieved mastery the same way Menelaos and Kristen did: by working with someone who knew more than you did. More specifically, by watching an expert for a bit, getting involved in easy, safe parts of the work, progressing to harder, riskier tasks with their guidance, and then finally starting to guide others. In surgery, this is called "see one, do one, teach one." But no matter what we call it, whether we even know it's going on, it's the same process—in pipefitting, midwifery, or carpentry, in an elementary school classroom or a high-energy-physics lab. And we have clear archaeological evidence of this process going back at least to the invention of language and the bow: about 160,000 years ago.[2]

Welcome to the expert-novice bond—a relationship that predates most of what we consider to be civilization. Experts can't do what they do without help. Novices want to help, and to learn. So they build a collaborative bond that's also the engine for building skill.

But wait, what about books? School? Workshops? Even Khan Academy or YouTube? Hasn't our increasingly connected, up-to-date, inexpensive, global academy taken center stage away from this old-school bond?

Nope. The research is clear on this, too—formal learning, at best, just gets you table stakes. It lets you start playing the game. But having conceptual knowledge *about* the work or doing practice exercises is very different from being able to do the work under pressure. To get there, most of us still rely primarily on collaboration with an expert. That relationship shapes our work so that we slowly, incrementally build layers of know-how that allow us to get results when it counts. If we step back from our own personal experience—if we look at human history as a long chain of relationships and interactions—this is how skill gets developed and passed between generations.

When something works this well, for this long, and for this many of us, we take it for granted. Question this and you might as well wonder if the sky is blue. But its success actually hinges on a set of essential criteria. If any of these is missing, skill dies, and the chain of excellence is at risk of being broken. And right now, as we transform more and more workplaces with intelligent technologies, these criteria are under threat.

FINDING THE SKILL CODE

Over the last ten years doing research on technology and work, I've found the hidden code that makes this relationship so powerful. When I say "code" here, I'm talking about something like the DNA of how we learn our most valuable skills. Our understanding of biology exploded when we discovered that it was all encoded in long strands of four simple amino acids, expressed in shorthand as ATCG.

The first key insight in this book is that the working relationship between experts and novices is a bundle of three Cs that humans need to develop mastery: challenge, complexity, and connection. Work near your limits, engage with the bigger picture, and build bonds of trust and respect. Like the four amino acids are to genetics, the three Cs are the basic building blocks of how we learn our most valuable skills. Take a look back and you will find them embedded in my tinsmithing encounter. You'll find them in your own journey to mastery, and in how you've helped others build mastery. But knowing the building blocks was just the beginning with genetics, and it's just the beginning with skill, too. You will learn that challenge, complexity, and connection need to occur in certain healthy—sometimes counterintuitive—ways to produce reliable skill. Sometimes these follow specific sequences that we're used to—that map with our beliefs of how skill development happens. But our world is changing. New sequences are emerging, others dying off. And one size doesn't fit every person, occupation, or organization. So, just like in biology, knowing this skill code empowers us not just to re-create the 160,000-year-old school, but to help us identify and preserve healthy skill building in any form it might take in this dizzying, modern world we're building for ourselves. That's because the skill code is technology agnostic: you can use it to look at any job involving any kind of tool. All this links to the second key insight: if we don't put this knowledge to use *right now*, our species is in deep trouble; we're handling intelligent technologies in ways that subtly degrade human ability.

James Watson and Francis Crick used a method called X-ray crystallography to get the first images of DNA, the structure and code for life.[3] I used a different method to get the equivalent for learning: organizational ethnography. This is a fancy term for field research, getting data from the real world by personally watching how and why businesses and organizations work—and, often, don't work. Asking a million questions of everyone involved. Pulling it all together systematically. Think of me as a scientific Mike Rowe from the show *Dirty Jobs* who sticks around about a thousand times longer, records and codes his observations, and focuses on jobs that depend on intelligent technologies like robotics and artificial intelligence (AI).

Clad head to toe in pale blue scrubs, I have stood in a university hospital operating room and watched with awe as a surgeon used a robot to cut inside a human body with millimeter-scale precision. I have hovered for hours in warehouses alongside temporary employees without high school diplomas as they found fixes for glitchy sorting robots that even the machine's designers couldn't puzzle out. For every research project, I spend one to two years watching, interviewing, and often working side by side with people who use robots to get their jobs done. And no matter what, I'm creating data as I go. Audio recordings. Photos and video. I can type at about the speed of conversation, too: for example, a four-hour surgical procedure produced about fifty pages of single-spaced, play-by-play detail on people, technology, talk, tasks, successes, failures—you name it. Ten years of this means I've personally observed and interviewed thousands of workers, managers, executives, and design engineers across disciplines and produced gigabytes of original data. A pharmacist in Akron, Ohio. A manager at a ghost kitchen in New York. A CEO in São Paolo, Brazil. A surgeon in Florida. They know me as the guy trying to learn how our work lives are changing as we put our latest technologies to use.

Each of my studies is designed to uncover success in conditions where we would expect failure. Deskilling jobs through automation? I'll be looking for a few deviants building skill anyway. Breaking human connection through remote work? I'm off to find the handful of workers who build great relationships anyway. Cutting back on maintenance on older equipment to prioritize the new? I'm on the hunt for the folks who keep ol' Bessy running and delivering results anyway. Finding these "positive needles" in the negative haystack of technological progress allows me to offer unique insights that can guide us as we try to navigate the future. As just one example, I am currently leading a team engaged in unprecedented—nationwide, multi-organizational, longitudinal—research on AI-enabled robots in e-commerce warehousing, looking for conditions in which front-line workers and their organizations adapt particularly well and rapidly to the introduction of these systems. Some of the people I study are ecstatic about new technologies. Some are worried. Many don't seem to notice or care. But regardless of attitude, occupation, industry, culture, or technology, I've found that the skill code is essential to their success—and that it is under threat.

I am not an innocent bystander in all this. I think that AI, robots, and related technologies are essential tools for advancing society. But I also share the fears of many others: that robots and AI will interfere with old ways of doing things with devastating consequences. I can't let that happen for skill. If intelligent technologies are going to truly help, then the expert-novice bond has to survive, too. And it's here that this book offers its third key insight: if it's going to flourish, the future of skill *needs* the very technologies we're concerned about. We need to use them to enrich, expand, and amplify skill development for everyone. We need to make them part of the solution, not the problem.

THE THREAT

In millions of workplaces, we're blocking the ability to master new skills because we are separating junior workers from senior workers, novices from experts, by inserting technology between them. In a grail-like quest to optimize productivity, we are disrupting the components of the skill code, taking for granted the necessary bundling of challenge, complexity, and connection that could help us build the skill we need to work with intelligent machines.

People often ask me: "Are robots going to take our jobs?" The immediate answer is yes: the best available research shows that for every robot that a firm buys, between three and six jobs are lost.[4] But there's a far more important question afoot than job losses. It's how many and what kinds of jobs we're *changing*. For over forty years, the research has shown one and only one pattern: when we put automation or even new technology to work, we don't eliminate many jobs, relative to the economy. Think tens of thousands. But many, many jobs change a little bit to accommodate the new way of working implied by the new technology. Think tens or even hundreds of millions. Which means that all those folks have to figure out the new way and get to a place where they can do it reliably. Smell skill development anywhere? Your nose is working. Learning is our critical challenge by a country mile because job change affects billions of us, and the pace of change is picking up.

Let's go back to Kristen in the OR to see how this is already playing out. Six months after her open surgical rotation, she wheels another prostate patient into the operating room where, this time, a hulking robot is waiting. The attending surgeon attaches the four-armed, thousand-pound robot to the patient. Then they both rip off their scrubs and head to control consoles fifteen feet away to do the whole operation "remotely."

Kristen just watches as her attending manipulates the robot's arms, retracting and dissecting tissue. Unlike the technologies that dot the history of surgery, using the robot makes it iPhone-easy for him to do the whole procedure himself. He knows Kristen needs practice; he wants to give her control. But he also knows she would be slower and make more mistakes, and she'd be going it alone. Slower means more time under anesthesia, which causes strokes. And mistakes mean blood loss, or worse. His patient comes first. So, Kristen has no hope of getting anywhere near those nerves during this rotation. In fact, she'll be lucky if she operates more than fifteen minutes during this four-hour procedure, and that will be on super-easy, safe stuff like cutting through fat. And when she does, he yells critiques at her across the room for all to hear, or, if she really slips up, he'll tap a touch screen and take control, banishing her to the sidelines, feeling like a kid in a dunce cap. No chance she's a better robotic surgeon after this procedure.

This adds up: Kristen and most of her fellow residents finish their training without much robotic confidence or surgical mastery. In her first independent job as a surgeon, Kristen sweats on the console. She stops, starts, pauses, and moves slowly. Burns and cuts a lot of extra tissue. There's a lot of tense silence and concerned looks between surgical staff. The patient loses about ten times more blood than they would have in the hands of Kristen's mentor, and what should have taken three hours takes seven. When I talked to Kristen's chief of surgery about what I witnessed in the robotic operating room, I asked him what he thought the implications of this new technique were for the profession. He had grave concerns. He pointed out that, while there were a few superstar robotic surgeons in the country, the vast majority of those operating with robots just didn't have the skill they should. He said, "I mean these guys can't do it. They haven't had any experience doing it. They watched it happen. Watching a movie doesn't make you an actor."

That got my attention.

Yet demand for robotic surgery is increasing rapidly; many hospitals have such a system and will pressure new surgeons like Kristen to use it. So, she will operate with it anyway. In 2019, *U.S. News & World Report* and *Wired* magazines independently investigated this and found robotic surgical training remained a "wild west," getting "terrible" results.[5] In 2022, *IEEE Spectrum*—the number one global popular magazine for engineers—found the same.[6] Many of us will go under the robotic knife with a surgeon who didn't get enough training, doesn't handle enough cases to keep their chops sharp, and doesn't feel all that confident when they sit down at the console.

Find this disturbing? I do, too. And it's only the beginning.

As with several other professions, surgery has been an early adopter of intelligent technologies, sitting at the very tip of the nose cone of the rocket we're building for ourselves, blasting into a brave new world. Now imagine this spreading across dozens of occupations and organizations. Then hundreds. Then around the globe. That's what's happening. Right now. I've taken a close look at the available data from dozens of those early-adopter domains and it shows we have already begun to break the learning encoded in apprenticeship-style interaction across a broad swath of professions.

Top corporate law firms are cutting costs aggressively, but they're spending more on one thing: technologies like AI "to support lawyers' workflow." Practically, this means automating document review. The firm doesn't involve or bill for that junior lawyer's time anymore, so senior experts do more, faster; clients pay less while the law firm can bill more with fewer staff so their profit goes up. But as a result, juniors become separated from seniors, losing visibility and exposure to their day-to-day work, and can't learn by helping. A recent Law.com review article sounded the alarm: "There is a whole generation of lawyers missing out on training and professional development."[7] Cops now get a predictive AI-assist for more productive beat assignments, and that means more time on crime, right?[8] Not for recruits, who have to fill out the paperwork that feeds these systems instead of spending time in the community with their mentors. In high finance, senior bankers' deepening investments in tools like FactSet and CapIQ now give them ready access to AI-enabled market analysis and firm valuations. So, 2021 saw a record $170 billion in profits. Except this automation changed workflows so that junior bankers spent most of their time on rote reports, away from senior bankers, who see "a weakening of (juniors) really understanding the trends and what's going on with the business."[9] From the cutting edge it's clear: the expert-novice connection is fraying where human and machine learning collide.

I have top-quality data on this problem from all sectors of the global economy. A significant chunk of this comes from more than ten years of my own research, but I've also gotten access to comparable data from other superb field researchers. Beyond the examples just above, here's a partial list of affected occupations that I'm adding to all the time: higher education, online labor platforms, chip design, journalism, data science, criminal justice, neonatal intensive care, public education, music composition, robotics, open innovation, aerospace engineering, ridesharing, long-haul trucking, bomb disposal, drone piloting, food service, secondary fulfillment, radiology, construction, wealth management, retail, automotive engineering, call center operations. In each of these settings there's a different intelligent technology at work, yet the same bonds are being severed. Almost every time.

This is a multitrillion-dollar problem.

Let's break this down: Recent estimates suggest that the skills gap—the skills that an industry needs, but can't find—costs us a trillion dollars in the global manufacturing industry alone.[10] Multiply that by every industry: for three years running, attracting and developing talent has topped the charts in the Conference Board's survey of the problems that keep CEOs up at night.[11] And workers, too: in one Deloitte survey of workers in 2020, 45 percent of respondents felt that their skills would be inadequate in three years.[12] In another by LinkedIn, a whopping 94 percent of respondents said they would stay at a company longer if it invested in their career development.[13] On top of all that, we're approaching this backward. Almost all of the half-trillion dollars we spent in 2020 on skills development went to formal training: in the classroom, online self-paced tutorials, or—more recently—video clips on a worker's cell phone.[14] Only a tiny fraction was devoted to the ubiquitous, informal bond at the foundation of our most valuable skills. And that pittance is being spent without an up-to-date understanding as to how that bond functions.

Why? The deal with AI is too good to pass up: these systems get better results by extending experts' impact. Try telling a senior journalist, mechanic, or executive to let now-optional trainees back in to struggle, add mistakes, and slow things down. Kristen's story—and dozens like hers, across industries, technologies, time, and roles—reveals what's at stake. In search of better results, more efficiency, and higher profits, we are designing these intelligent technologies, directing them, and making choices about what research to invest in. And we're paying a hidden, multitrillion-dollar price for it.

Technologies, techniques, and skills come and go, and even the way the traditional expert-novice relationship plays out has shifted over time to accommodate the increasingly complex skills required to get results. Menelaos couldn't use something called a "smartphone" to call, email, or send photos to Stephanos from the markets in Rome, after all. But we've always had time to adapt. Critically, we've done that through expert-novice collaboration itself—to build the know-how required to stitch together new technologies, techniques, and working relationships. Now this kind of learning is a real struggle, and it's getting harder. This systematic assault is a death knell for expert-novice collaboration as we've known it for centuries, and with it goes the valuable skill that flows from following the skill code of challenge, complexity, and connection. The next generation of skilled workers is getting gutted, and organizations are hollowing themselves out as a result. If we're not careful, our individual and collective adaptability could fade, just when we need it most.

REWORKING THE SKILL CODE

But this is not a "the sky is falling" book. I bring good news from the front lines. In my research, I've gone to great lengths to find people who are defying the odds and getting good results. Faced with the erosion of the expert-novice bond, some people are finding a new way that the rest of us and our organizations can learn from.

Take Beth, another surgical resident who—on paper—was in the same spot Kristen was in. They were in the same top hospital. She came from a similar medical school, with similar courses. She had the same attending surgeon. She got similar patients. And maybe most important, she got the same formal training in robotic surgery.

But right away I could tell something different was going on. Beth didn't feel frustrated, bored, and shut out of the learning process like Kristen did. And that's because she wasn't: every time she came into the OR the attending let her operate between ten and fifty times as long as Kristen. And where Kristen looked like a baby foal learning to walk, Beth was *good*. She operated quickly and decisively. She had insightful questions for her attending. She could even issue simple requests to the operating team while operating with the robot—something Kristen forgot was even possible while she was sweating away in the console.

What was going on here?

It turns out that during medical school, Beth was a bit of a rebel, but one with a cause. She had a habit of cutting anatomy and physiology labs to spend time in the operating room with a senior robotic surgeon. Then she landed a research assistant role in a lab developing a new robotic surgical technique. On top of this, she spent hundreds of hours in her early residency reviewing videos of robotic surgery when she should have been spending time with her patients or sleeping. The result of all this insatiable, off-script learning was that the first time she sat down in a console to operate as a second-year resident—earlier than most, because she was already asking smart questions—she looked like she knew what she was doing. She got to operate more. And when her rotation to the local US Department of Veterans Affairs hospital came up, the attending assumed she knew more than she did and was more inclined to let her operate, even wondering if he could learn a thing or two. Over time, Beth kept getting better and better the longer she was behind the console. As a result, she became one of the most skilled residents in robotic surgery. How had she done this?

By bending, breaking, and rewriting the rules—by becoming a shadow learner.

When the expert-novice bond is broken, my research shows that a small minority of people like Beth learn anyway. Close to a hundred years ago, the sociologist Robert Merton showed that when legitimate means are no longer effective for achieving a valued goal, a few people engage in deviant behavior to achieve it regardless.[15] Skill—perhaps the ultimate occupational goal—is no exception: given the extreme barriers to skill building that I've discovered, it's no surprise that people have had to find transgressive ways to learn key skills and keep their learning edge razor-sharp. In fact, studying this closely revealed that expertise only sometimes tracks formal hierarchy: colleagues and I have found senior members of an occupation learning new technologies from novices! This is what I mean by "shadow": deviants gaining mastery outside the bright lights of convention and its rules.

In the pages ahead, I'm going to reveal what shadow learners can teach us about preserving healthy challenge, complexity, and connection—the three essential elements of the skill code. We'll examine each C in detail and see that the subtleties matter. Too much challenge, too fast, for example, and we don't learn much. Too much "help" from an expert keeps us away from that learning edge, and so it limits us the same way. That's not to say shadow learners have a perfect recipe for success—their solutions are at best semi-ethical hacks that wouldn't scale. But these practices are precious clues for the journey ahead.

It's often not appropriate to re-create traditional apprenticeships anymore—our world is changing too fast, and there are too many kinds of work for a uniform, complicated solution anyway. That's why the skill code is important: it breaks skill development down into more elemental units that apply to all of us, everywhere, all the time. Knowing about these three Cs—and what it looks like when they're working well—gives you the perspective and clear tactics to keep this bond healthy and the skill flowing. These lessons apply immediately to your work, whether you're a novice seeking to build mastery, an expert seeking to build it in others, a leader trying to build rich skills into your organization, or a technologist trying to build skill-enhancing tools. That's right: intelligent technologies can—and in many places, must—be part of the skill solution. You may be tempted to conclude we're living in a "John Henry" moment, where it's techno-productivity versus human ability. But my fresh findings show we can transcend this dilemma: in many cases we can get new, breathtaking results only by augmenting the skill code with intelligent technologies.

But no matter the role of technology in your work, this book also offers guidance for your organizational, professional, and personal skills journey derived from rigorous research on these "shadow learners" across dozens of occupations—how to adapt and preserve the skill code even when the way we work changes almost beyond recognition. You can trust this guidance—it got results for workers who could have been shamed or fired for trying it out. It had to work to be worth the risk.

These hard-won lessons give us a clear set of tools to preserve and enhance what's best about traditional apprentice-style collaboration. These tactics—and the skill code that underwrites them—are crucial for the road ahead. We have a huge opportunity—and a dire need—to recode our work and our technologies so they enhance challenge, complexity, and connection and the valuable skills that flow from them. We need to seize it before it's too late.

CHAPTER TWO

CHALLENGE

It took Andre six years to work his way into his job: deputy chef at a three-star Michelin steakhouse. This is just one level below chef de cuisine, the head of the house. The pay is solid, but the main thing that got him there was the work itself. The head prep—the informal title of the person who manages all food preparation work in the kitchen and practically works for Andre—is waiting for him when he pulls around the back of the restaurant to kick off the day, Red Bull in hand: "Hair of the dog, chef?" he chuckles. They part ways at the door and Andre heads to the office to check over the closing manager's notes and solidify his prep list for the day. He walks around the dining room, turning on all the lights, and takes a good, hard look around to check on the closers' and cleaners' work from the night before. Then he addresses the morning crew in the kitchen: "Good morning, chefs. Are we going to be ready today?" "Yes, chef" comes the emphatic, unified reply. "Let's get to it, then," he says. They break and get to work, because it's time for prep: ingredients, of course, but also things like knife sharpening, getting salad plates in the cooler, half-pan backups on the line, and firing up the soup wells—there is no room for error in things like cross-contamination, wrong temperatures, dull knives, and customer allergy accommodations. So, if he and the crew don't do all this before the waitstaff shows up, he's in trouble.

When they do, the time flies by as he almost jogs around the kitchen to assist with prep and stocking across stations: grill, fry, sauté, boil, pantry, dish tank, the list goes on. Since he curates the menu, recipes, ingredients, design, and presentation, all this work has to be done in very particular ways, and he spot-checks it throughout the day. "One forty-nine, chef!?" he yells as he strides by the soup station. "Yes, chef!" comes the reply, after a quickly dunked thermometer. "Chef, is this fine enough?" he says to Kate, a prep, pointing to the diced onions in front of her. "No, chef!" she replies, then takes a fierce second look after he walks away. This kind of tight supervision might not be *fun* for Kate and the rest of the staff, exactly, but they trust in Andre's standards. As the evening winds down, he can let his steward and line cook handle the last few orders and start breaking down the line and cleaning. Andre takes this time to set the general manager up for a smooth closing. Before he clocks out, he takes a run through his work email to answer applications, vendor advertisements, and distributor promotions. It's one heck of a ride, took a lot of Red Bull, some screaming and smokes in the alley, but the food quality for the shift? Perfection.

He can't quite explain it, but being a shoulder-to-shoulder, moment-to-moment part of a team that serves up a profitable, quality product every day, straight through the rush . . . well, that's just a thrill. It takes a lot of skill and earns a lot of respect. Sure, he had a fair amount of setup work to do, but it was manageable.

He had meaningful time to connect with vendors and front-of-house staff ahead of time, to chew the fat with prep cooks or the pastry chef as he worked at a steady pace. But he was generally in constant motion when the night got started, and that's what he liked. His expertise was needed for everything from changing settings on equipment like a nitrogen freezer, to scrambling for an improvised mix of ice, cleaning pads, and gauze when someone cut their hand, to maintaining a smooth, relaxed flow of communication across the job functions in the kitchen. He had to pay fierce attention; he had to be ready. Being a deputy chef was dirty, dangerous, and therefore challenging work, and he loved it.

But in his early days coming up through food prep, he wouldn't have lasted five minutes without *his* deputy chef, Jane. Before his first few days apprenticing "up" for her role, they met ahead of time, chatted, and Jane laid out a plan: Andre would do easier, more peripheral tasks first, taking his lead from Jane, and they'd debrief over break. Jane shot him straight, propped him up, and then threw more difficult work at him—a bit more than he thought he could handle. And Andre knew that when it was game time, Jane wasn't coming to his rescue. So after he mastered prep and showed interest in inventory, she tagged him up with her purchasing guy and introduced him to the appliance maintenance tech. The week after that it was the stations upstream and downstream of his station. Then he set his own stretch goal of cutting his prep time by 25 percent and got her approving nod when he hit it. Shifts flew by, and he sweated through his whites most days, but sooner than he expected, Andre was taking the lead and Jane took a back seat.

A healthy serving of challenge—cooked up by an expert chef—was just the right nutrition for Andre's development. All the research points to the same conclusion: we don't get valuable skill without healthy challenge, and the expert-novice bond is made to deliver it.

WE NEED HEALTHY CHALLENGE TO LEARN

Decades of research on education, motor skill, the psychology of learning, the sociology of occupations—and now even neurobiology and artificial intelligence—confirm that we're all like Andre. We learn best when we get *healthy* challenge: too much, and we burn out. Too little and we stagnate.

Take, for example, the fascinating research on "desirable difficulties." Curious about how students learned and retained information, Robert Bjork, a psychologist at the University of California, Los Angeles, initiated this work in 1994.[1] He knew students crammed for tests by rereading their notes or a textbook. And he knew that from the learner's point of view, rereading *felt* like it worked: all the material makes just a bit more sense on that third or fifth read through. Who wants to use flash cards, anyway? It's almost literally painful to stop yourself from flipping the dang thing over, to sweat out the answer, pace around, yell at a wall, and then finally either give up or blurt it out. Rereading must work better than the strain of trying to remember, right? Nope. Bjork found this learner's intuitive preference is flat wrong. His early work—and the dozens of studies from many other researchers after that—showed that this additional effort and more complicated processing involved in quizzing yourself was worth it. Yes, it takes longer, and the learner doesn't feel as confident, but they retain more and develop a greater sense of mastery in the long haul. The difficulty needs to be desirable in two very different ways: First, the learner has to want to be able to complete the task. They have to care. But second, the intensity of the difficulty must be objectively desirable for their learning: they build more sustainable skill if they encounter it than they would without it.

Two other researchers, Mark Guadagnoli and Timothy Lee, built on Bjork's work. They proposed that to understand learning and skill, you had to understand the relationship between the task difficulty and the learner's preexisting skills.[2] They suggested that learners would do best when they worked at their "optimal challenge point." This is a point where you build the most long-term skill and confidence while still performing well on the task in the short run. Just like many things in life, this is a Goldilocks phenomenon: not too difficult, not too easy. Performance will be hard, and you won't do your best, but the task will seem doable, and you can adjust the difficulty to suit your increasing skill. When Andre first started working the grill and range, for instance, he could just manage three dishes at a time—watching and testing each for crispiness, scent, texture, listening to each one sizzle—it was intelligible, and he kept it together, but keeping all three on track was a struggle. As the days wore on, however, he started to tend to more burners, because, well, he just *knew* what was going on with three dishes. He was used to it. He could understand the symphony of sounds and smells. Eventually he handled an entire range top of pans and cuts of meat, all at once. It never felt easy, there were always minor, recoverable screwups, and he was always sweating—but he could do it, and he was learning.

This link between struggle and skill shows up in dozens of studies, and this research is getting more convincing and more precise. Physical therapists Kazunori Akizuki and Yukari Ohashi, looking for the right amount of challenge for their recovering patients, gave participants a posture control task: stand up straight on an unstable surface.[3] They assessed how difficult the task was by taking samples of participants' saliva and testing for alpha amylase, an enzyme that correlates very well with stress. They also administered the NASA Task Load Index, a well-validated measure of task difficulty.[4] Like the many studies before and after, subjects learned better the more they were stressed and challenged, up to a point—81 percent above normal alpha amylase readings and a 51.5 on the NASA scale—but their learning went down after that. Overdrill your recruits or exclude your interns and you will probably hurt skill, too. And that's to say nothing of any technological gas you've thrown on those fires, whether it be remote work or expert-enhancing AI.

CHALLENGE IS BETTER WITH A GUIDE

While we *can* go it alone when it comes to challenge, the research clearly shows that we often *shouldn't.* As you get into a bit of hot water while trying to get better, you have to focus. Intently. And it's often harder than we expect to maintain that focus and self-control in the right ways for the right amount of time to get better. With an expert's help, we can take on more challenge and get more skill out of it.

This conclusion is central to the heap of rigorous research on how kids build skill. Early in the twentieth century, but in only the last few years of his short life, psychologist Lev Vygotsky introduced a powerful idea, which he called "a zone of proximal development."[5] Vygotsky spent many hours studying the effects of school instruction. He found that whatever the lesson—say reading—kids could do some things unaided, couldn't do some things at all, but there was an interesting middle ground where they could do some tasks with guidance. He called this interesting middle a zone of proximal development and inspired generations of educational researchers to study how teachers could most effectively help kids enter this zone and get the most from it. Self-directed learning was all the rage back then—this was when Montessori and Waldorf-style schools surged in popularity—and he believed there was an important role for just the right kind of guidance on tasks.

The decades of research that followed tell a pretty straightforward tale: when students got the hardest tasks they could handle *with guidance*, they learned more and built more confidence in the long run than they did if they struggled on their own. Benjamin Bloom, an educational researcher at the University of Chicago, showed the world that when an average student got held to this standard via one-on-one tutoring, they improved to the 95th percentile of achievement.[6] Getting there took starting with the basics—say how to hold a knife to chop produce and the best way to sear steak—and progressed to complicated tasks like making a sauce. In the late 1970s, educational researchers Jerome Bruner, David Wood, and Gail Ross coined the term *scaffolding* to describe this activity—the parsing out of challenge over time, in a manner that would keep learners engaged.[7] Most any elementary school teacher has probably heard of scaffolding, but even if they haven't, their curriculum and classroom experience is probably based on it. Their very first study in this domain—of three- to five-year-olds trying to assemble a block pyramid with a helping adult present—revealed several critical features of this activity that have stood the test of time.

The "how" of scaffolding is spread across this and the following two chapters: it's that central to skill. Here we're focused on challenge, which can leave novices bewildered, demotivated, and angry, so frustration management is the scaffolding tactic that matters most.

An expert can help you take on more challenge and build more skill than you could without their help. But to do that, you're stepping into task territory that's significantly more difficult than you might otherwise be able to handle, so you're at risk of feeling more incompetent, too. Hitting an 80-mph fastball instead of a 50-mph one. Making a soufflé instead of scrambled eggs. Facilitating an executive off-site, not a midlevel team meeting. The scaffolding research helps us see that experts can help you cope with related frustration in two ways: preemptively, by indicating the payoff of the coming struggle, and reactively, by reminding us how far we're stretching. In the baseball example, the preemptive move might be "Want to play on the varsity team in high school? You have to be able to hit pitches at least this fast." That gets the novice motivated. The reactive one—after a first hit that went nowhere—might be "Great. You can now officially hit a foul ball in the majors. Just keep making contact for a bit." That reminds the novice their failure is actually also a success.

To step away from matters of motivation and emotion, we also know that scaffolding only works well when both the expert and the novice have a solid, shared understanding of the goal. Andre got a lot more out of his blood, sweat, and tears because he and his mentors were clear on the outcomes he was trying to produce. Smooth sauces. Sharp knives. Elegant plating. No one had to wonder. The opposite would be true for an administrative assistant in a publishing company who is trying to learn proposal review from an expert who's never shared a great one. Shared clarity on outcomes is essential. What does success look like (and smell like, in the case of Andre)? We also know good scaffolding is highly individualized. Even for the same task in the same conditions, every learner is at a different point in their journey, has certain preferences and tendencies, is having a certain kind of day, and has differing potential life trajectories. For some prep cooks in Andre's kitchen, filleting salmon is a necessary terror en route to working in pastry, while for others it's what they've been waiting for. If he doesn't understand this, Andre might overextend the first and bore the second. So, the scaffolder—the expert with more capability—has to understand each novice's capabilities and goals, so they can tune their support appropriately.

But we have also learned that different situations call for different scaffolding approaches, regardless of the learner involved. For example, when the task is very well structured—where the next thing the learner is going to struggle with is usually the same— approaches to scaffolding can be, too. In school, this might be reading a passage of text or doing arithmetic. In carpentry, it might be hammering a nail or cutting a two-by-four on a table saw. The point is: the challenge and the goal aren't going to vary much, so guidance can be more directive, focused, and closed-ended. When the task is very unstructured—creating a piece of art or learning to cooperate—scaffolders have to be ready to pivot in many directions. If someone is learning to cooperate, it might become evident that they're struggling with giving feedback, structuring conversations with agendas, listening with empathy, or seeking input from everyone. The list of challenges is practically infinite, so guidance on how to engage with it needs to be less directive, fluid, and openended.

Finally, just as the metaphor implies, scaffolding is temporary. If you've got an expert helping you struggle near the edge of your capacity, eventually it will get easier: you'll have built skill. As this happens, the expert should back away and let the novice handle the challenges that they can and should handle for themselves. Allan Collins, John Seely Brown, and Susan Newman called this "fading" in their 1986 book on apprenticeship.[8] Andre does this intuitively: he starts that eager filleter with skinning and deboning, and he stands by to watch for egregious errors and offer feedback. Copper river salmon's not cheap, after all. But once she starts to get the hang of it, he challenges her to do it in smoother motions, fewer cuts, and with less waste. And he steps away. He's letting the old scaffolding fade and bringing in new scaffolding for new challenges, and the prep chef takes on more and more responsibility for the work. This recipe extends to experts and novices everywhere.

CHALLENGE IS A CONTACT SPORT

So, fine, you've got an expert offering you superb scaffolding. You're facing challenges you couldn't face on your own. Good enough for skill? No way! If we took it at face value, the scaffolding literature makes healthy challenge seem like a predictable resource that can be thoroughly managed by you and a thoughtful guide. The welter of normal work makes a mockery of that pristine image: you often don't get dedicated attention, you have to share resources with other novices, you have to produce output that's judged by multiple people, and you have to collaborate in unexpected ways on the daily. School is like that, too. We can thank Benjamin Bloom for that knowledge. He isn't famous for the power of tutoring. If he's well known anywhere, it's for naming the "two sigma problem": the fact that we can't possibly provide one-on-one support, and we need to make group-based methods work better.[9] Counting on customized, steady scaffolding is not a realistic way of securing the healthy challenge that will help you build a skill you can rely on to deliver results under pressure at work—private lessons weren't what allowed deputy chef Andre to respond productively to a rush of orders or a power outage. For him and for us all, challenge is a contact sport.

Research into what we might call "real-world skill" started in the 1940s and '50s. From cops to doctors, copy machine techs to midwives and everything in between, researchers wanted to know: How do you get into occupations? How do you get ahead in them? And what's the role of skill in these stories? Answering questions like these drove researchers to adapt anthropological methods to understand how members of a group—an occupation, for example—built skill and got ahead. Across the world, professional researchers lived and worked side by side with members of these occupations, shadowing them as they joined and matured in these communities. They went through the same processes, in many cases getting the same credentials, doing the same work, and building the same skills. We know what they learned because they wrote it all down: on smoke breaks from working on the line, in the back of a police cruiser, in the resident rest area, and even in the bathroom. John Van Maanen (a member of my dissertation committee at MIT) was at the vanguard of this movement and has a roomful of hand-scrawled notes to show for it. In fact, "The

Asshole"—one of his famous papers on how cops mete out street justice—instantly convinced me I was meant to join this tribe.[10] Less than a year later, at 3:19 in the morning, I found myself furiously typing notes on "robot rounds" in a postsurgical ICU. I gathered data on the night shift in that ICU for fourteen months, asking what difference a telepresence robot made for how senior docs checked on their patients—and what happened to medical residents' learning as a result. I'm one of many researchers who have done this kind of work, so as the decades have rolled on, we've gotten dozens of accounts of how people entered and got ahead in a diverse range of occupations, and a coherent picture has emerged.

In fact, Jean Lave and Etienne Wenger, an anthropologist and computer scientist who had done their own field study of apprenticeships among traditional tailors in Africa, were the first to formally recognize that learning happened in the same way across all these studies.[11] They helped us see that to begin your journey in an occupation—let's take finance—you had to build some sort of generalist knowledge. You learned basic accounting and budgeting, you learned about basic analysis, statements, and software, and you learned the various specialties within the occupation and the problems they focused on: corporate finance and shareholder value, venture capital and new venture funding, and so on. And you might have gotten some offline practice in basic techniques like cash flow analysis and ledger analysis. But everyone would know that all of this was the price of entry, not your ticket to membership. To become a CPA and a financial planner—to be granted that title and a license to work on those problems—you got involved in practicing financial planners' work, helping them in limited ways in the beginning, more complicated ways as you went on, and ultimately helped to mentor newbies as you were about to complete your training. Similarly, Andre the chef started in prep—"simply" chopping produce and boning meat on demand for the head prep. Then he set his own plans and space for his work, and finally got involved in ordering for prep just as he started to oversee newbie preppers fresh off the street. When the broader community of social scientists took stock of facts like this, they saw the same patterns in the many studies of what's known as "occupational socialization," or the process of how new members became competent, accepted members of an occupation.

Beyond helping us to see these general patterns, all this research—nearly eighty years of rich study across many dozens of work contexts and occupations—shows that healthy challenge is absolutely essential to skill development. It's clear that new recruits compete for the chance to do challenging work *near the edge* of their capacity with an expert present. Cadets want to walk difficult beats with their senior officer. Apprentice doulas want to take the lead when the mother is in labor. Butchers' assistants want to be guided as they deal with prime cuts of meat. New helpers in a distillery want to see if they can smell and taste the quality of the mash in front of the chief distiller. The medical residents I studied in an ICU wanted to piece together a tricky bedside diagnosis with their attending. It's not just because they are trying to look competent to impress their mentor: when they deal with tough work, they make mistakes, move slowly, ask "stupid" questions, and need to repeat themselves. Obviously, they might look better if they didn't struggle. But they realize a critical fact of occupational life: problems and practice are a scarce and critical resource.

This isn't just because most work is routine. When short-term results are a priority, many people—a boss, a customer, a colleague—will prefer you to perform at your best. I found this myself in my own studies of the transition to robotic surgery. Kristen, and residents like her, made mistakes and moved slower than experts. Even though almost all these mistakes were minor and recoverable, senior docs had a hard time letting residents struggle—the patient's body and sometimes the hospital's profitability came first. The same went for Andre in the kitchen—he knew that trying out a new technique couldn't come at the expense of a full prep bin. The trouble—evident in the research on occupations, work, and reliability, actually—is that we have a very hard time distinguishing between mistakes that would cause an unrecoverable catastrophe and those that can be easily addressed.[12] Up close it all feels *bad*. So even without the technological threat to novice participation I identify in this book, others will often have an incentive to keep you *away* from struggle. You get ahead by solving harder problems, though, both by building skill and through the respect that earns. So sometimes you have to invent or fight for opportunities to struggle and fail.

Part of the tussle for challenge is about making time away from work for what K. Anders Ericsson called "deliberate practice"—repeated, high-concentration practice outside your comfort zone.[13] Ericsson was perhaps *the* leading psychologist to study skill directly, inspiring hundreds of studies in this area. He and many colleagues showed through numerous studies that top performers take the next thing they can't do, break it down, and practice a single, difficult component of it until it flows—an aspiring jazz pianist who eventually wants to jam on a Miles Davis tune will first practice their chromatic minor scales over and over, up and down until they can run them at high speed without thinking, for example. In other cases, making your own challenge means finding opportunities to handle uncomfortably challenging "live fire" work. Either way, total failure doesn't teach you much. The evidence across all these studies shows that the tasks worth fighting for are those where the expert needs you, and you need them, but you're sweating it. And this is a critical part of the threat that comes from separating experts and novices through technologies like AI and robotics: the farther away from an expert you are, the farther away from healthy challenge, too.

If we look a bit further outside the confines of our conscious experience, we find even more support for this "healthy challenge for learning" idea. This shows up when we look at the connection between the nervous system and memory, for example. Researchers have found that stress interfaces with the part of the brain that generates catecholamines—neurotransmitters ranging from noradrenaline to dopamine—that facilitate "fight or flight" responses,[14] as well as attention and memory-encoding processes.[15] These studies show that we learn *better* when we experience stress just before, during, and after we are encoding information. So low stress surrounding an event means lower quality learning and memory about it. The flip is also true: if we learn in stressful situations, our brain and nervous system make it stick. Amazingly, this work also shows us that stress doesn't enhance learning about everything going on during a stressful task—it specifically enhances memory for material that is related to the task itself. And finally, foundational research on "incidental learning" (the semiconscious by-product of just doing a task a lot) has shown that there is an "optimal intermediate degree" of stress for memory formation.[16] This kind of learning is very strong: researchers have also found that we're much more resistant to misinformation about an event if we experienced it while stressed.[17] Andre certainly wouldn't believe you if you told him that it was okay to drop frozen items into the deep fryer: he remembers that day it happened because they exploded. He'll never forget *that* lesson.

There's a final, surprising source of evidence that challenge is core to learning: machine learning (aka AI). In fact, the last fifteen years of progress in AI have hinged on making it *harder* for these systems to learn, not easier. Here we have the advent of "adversarial training," for example, where computer scientists realized the best learning came from a strict diet of email spam.[18] The state of the art used to be systems that learned from everything—the easy, safe messages mixed with the difficult, dangerous messages. Then some in the AI community saw another way forward: they built systems that relied *entirely* on attacks as training data. Forget the easy stuff, just give me challenge! But systems like these still required a steady diet of new spam and still had a fundamental problem: they could only stop something they'd seen before. The more recent upgrade was to skip the wait for real toxic spam by building Generative Adversarial Networks (or GANs) to automate the "learning through challenge and failure" process. GANs involve a pair of algorithms in a competition.[19] A "discriminator" tries to label real versus fake messages, and a "generator" creates fake messages that are indistinguishable from the real thing. The discriminator gets fed a mix of real messages and the generator's fakes, and both get digital rewards or penalties when they "win" in this competition. This struggle drives both systems to previously impossible performance levels—and, importantly, an ability to respond productively to surprising challenges that just wasn't there before. These GANs learn through challenge, and our inboxes are saved.

All this sound familiar?

It would to Andre. He might be having the strange realization that he and AI are much more alike than he expected. But looking over this and all the research in this chapter, he'd have a deeper, more significant revelation: he's been lucky when it comes to challenge in his career so far. Even when his early prep tasks were easy, his time for them was short: chop produce before cooking starts. That time pressure was a gift: he could only do the job with quality if he got better, and he *wanted* to get better. So he focused, competed with the clock, and built skill. But the work itself—while intense during a shift—provided natural breaks. Some mindless leek dicing allowed for a breather after dealing with a new sauce, for example. And while he didn't always have great mentorship—some of the sous chefs above him were explosive and cruel—most of the time he had someone nearby who knew more and would help him out if he yelled for it. Then it was literally back to the cutting board to practice while getting his job done. And he didn't have anyone micromanaging him or rescuing him from any chance to mess up—the mentality in the kitchen was you either handle your job or you are out. That felt right to him, and so did the challenge.

FINDING CHALLENGE IN YOUR ORGANIZATION, OCCUPATION, AND WORK

Before you can pursue and protect healthy challenge, you need to be able to identify it. This sounds easy: it's just when someone's struggling, right?

Sort of. But that's like saying nitrogen is good for plants. Too much, or given in the wrong form, and it has terrible or neutral consequences. Challenge is the same: sometimes struggle is terrible for learning—and lots of other things. It needs to occur in the right amounts and in the right way for people to build skill on the job and help others do the same.

The specific characteristics of healthy challenge are peppered throughout this chapter. Let's pull them together here in a ten-point checklist for easy reference. You're facing healthy challenge when:

- ❑ You have work that's near—not way below or beyond— your capabilities. You'll know because it requires near-total focus, and you can perform this work well, but not at your best.
- ❑ The level of challenge isn't constant: parts of the work are straightforward to you.
- ❑ You want to get better at this work, and you don't want to fail.

❑ You still fail in small ways, every time you try—part of your challenge involves recovering from small failures.

❑ You have time to recover—either during straightforward work or off the job.

❑ You have enough work in front of you to face similar challenges once you have recovered from the first burst. You need repeat opportunities to learn.

❑ You create, seek, and even compete for challenge when it's in limited supply.

❑ In return, experts make sure you're on the same page about the goal, and help you manage frustration— proactively by reminding you of the payoff, and reactively by reminding you how far you're stretching.

❑ They retune their guidance to your developing skill and adjust their approach to match the work: when the task is highly structured, so is the mentorship. When it's very unstructured, their methods are more fluid.

❑ Finally, experts reserve their help for tasks that are just a bit more challenging than you could handle on your own—they stop helping you cope with challenge as you start being able to take it on yourself.

You can use this checklist to assess your organization, occupation, and work and to think about what you need to change—or keep the same—to get the skills you need. You can share it with others and help them do the same. Cultivating healthy challenge is a skill set in and of itself. And building these skills may be your highest-leverage option if you want to boost your own, your team's, or your organization's effectiveness.

The way you apply this checklist will depend on your role.

If you're a leader, take a close look at your organization with this checklist in hand. To do this broadly, you probably need to commit resources: either hire or refocus people to understand the state of challenge in your organization, and the conditions that led to that. Where do processes degrade, prevent, or limit healthy challenge? Why? Does your onboarding process, for example, subtly nudge new employees away from challenging assignments or provide excessive support? And on the other hand, you need to ask: Where do those processes enhance healthy challenge? Might a "broken" job rotation system actually leave specialists to struggle in healthier ways? If so, you might "fix" the process—say by eliminating bureaucracy or ensuring that candidates have good jobs to rotate into—without losing that benefit. You might then "break" other processes in similar ways: if limited supervision actually gave new, valuable space for struggle, you might find comparable ways to cut back on supervision elsewhere, too. You might also ask yourself whether the guidance and training you're providing is coming in the right form, at the right time. It will often make the most sense to focus your challenge assessment in the areas where skilled action and talent development are most valuable to the enterprise. In other cases, it will make sense to focus on universal processes like onboarding or rotations. The key is to get a clearer picture. All of this includes you: no doubt you and your team are healthily challenged while also having areas to improve on. Showing you're looking into this can set a powerful example.

Of course, you should also dedicate resources to building healthy challenge—for you, your team, your colleagues, and your organization. In many cases this will *reduce* cost because it will mean stopping or eliminating something. Take a close look at bureaucracy, for example: it can evolve to the point where risk, urgency, and challenge are viewed as the enemy. Eliminating a tool, a form, a meeting, a process, or a role might just reinvigorate the work with some challenge. More positively, you can include the checklist for healthy challenge in your goal setting and performance review tools—if everyone is measured against how well they target and preserve healthy challenge, they'll start to take action.

If you're on an occupational certification board—a group that sets standards for membership in an occupation or profession—you're a critical arbiter of what "good work" looks like. You decide who can legally work as an electrician, doctor, CPA, architect, lawyer, and so on, and you decide what folks have to do to keep current, specialize, or prove they're doing quality work. You set the tone and the rules, and you influence policy so that your occupation's members are seen as legitimate, capable servants of society. Do those norms and rules perpetuate any threats to healthy challenge that are cropping up in your members' work? Do your policies for certification and training with new tools recognize threats to challenge and hedge against them? To get ahead of the technothreats in this book, an electrician certification board might create rules that limit the kinds of help that auditors, proctors, and mentors can offer when newer members are struggling to learn, and that expand the risk that members have to face as they practice, even though new technologies are reshaping the work. They might also watch out for making up too many new rules, given that new technologies are giving them so much new information about novice work performance. Otherwise, there's risk that their policies would become "tighter," making it harder for new members to struggle, make minor mistakes, and recover.

And if this is personal—if your skill or ability to help others learn is the story—you can use this list to think through what you need to change to improve outcomes for you and those trying to learn. Take an honest look at your work. Does it pass the healthy challenge checklist? For example, do you have a manager or mentor who engages in what I call "helicopter teaching," essentially keeping you away from struggling and performing less than your very best? And did technology have anything to do with that? A short- and mid-haul delivery driver might look at whether increased digital connectivity with management and corporate algorithms meant depriving them of the "interesting" challenges in their work. Or, on the upside, how these systems might be giving them challenge via a host of new interfaces and interaction modalities where before they just had a speedometer and GPS. But overall, they'd make healthy challenge their project. You should, too. Finally, if you're the expert, take a look at how you're collaborating with those trying to learn. Do they have healthy challenge? A manager in a social service agency might consider what working remotely is doing to new clinicians' and caseworkers' ability to handle the intensity of in-person therapeutic work. Or, like the palliative care doc I interviewed, you might look into whether using telepresence for patient sessions actually tunes down the challenge to a healthier range for new members, before they shift to in-person work.

You might not have the burn and slash scars on your forearms that Andre does to show for his rise through a Michelin-star kitchen, but when it comes to challenge and skill, you're just like him. We all are. Take a moment and think about something valuable that you can reliably do well under pressure. Ride a bike. Host a party. Text on a phone. Learn your way around a new town. Write an Excel macro. Whatever it is, when you do it, other folks go "wow," and you're not afraid to fail. Now you know: Your confidence and expertise are products of difficulty. You rose to the challenge. But you also know that—like Andre—you're lucky. The challenge could have been too intense or not intense enough. You might not have gotten the breaks you needed to recoup and reflect. You might not have cared enough to try harder and even invent your own challenges. You might not have gotten the right kinds of support. The list goes on. But it's not vague, or infinite. It has ten items, you know how they work, and they're in your hands.

We're just getting started on the skill code, however. A second careful look at your or Andre's story reveals that this first C, challenge, wasn't the whole show—we all need healthy complexity and connection, too. To learn about these, let's leave Andre and the kitchen and visit Sita at her warehousing job.

CHAPTER THREE

COMPLEXITY

It took Sita five years to land her job as a shift supervisor at a Baltimore-area warehouse that assembles goods like subscription boxes and repair kits. Only the CEO and the facility manager sit above her in this family-owned organization. So her rise means she can independently support her three kids and send money back to her family in Nepal every month. Six days a week, she rolls up to the building at six thirty in the morning for a circle-up meeting in the middle of the floor with her area "supes"—the people who oversee the six to eight different customer jobs the company has going at any one time. Today it's customers asking for cardboard spice rack assembly, subscription pet treat boxes, tile display samples, green lighting kits for corporate electricians, and toenail polish filling. As they review input from the graveyard shift, Sita asks them what they've noticed since yesterday morning and tells one supe to double-check inbound product for quality; then the group solidifies the plan for the day. Then they break, and each area supe leads their own local huddle with the temp workers who started clocking in to the building at 6:45. But Sita's already on the move.

She walks briskly to the subscription box line, where she checks on the status of an order. It's a new customer with exacting standards, so she'll be there until the crew gets things "smooth." Her head is on a swivel—scanning everything from the cleanliness of the floor to the state of the equipment, every PC screen, each person and their activity, the pallets in receiving and shipping— and listening carefully throughout. It's her way of keeping her finger on the pulse of the building. Once Sita gets to the box line, she walks around and pitches in as temp workers break open big pallets of pet toys and treats each morning, working together to set up the tables where they will be sorted, fold the cardboard boxes they will eventually go in, sort them into three-by-two-foot, color-coded plastic totes and set these totes next to a mechanical conveyor. She works alongside Garrett, the "replen" person who keeps each bin full, and nudges him to look at the packaging for inbound pallets. Then she moves on to the person who feeds the completed boxes into a taping and printing machine, then the line lead who enters throughput and quality data into a nearby PC.

To Sita, every job, every detail, every surprise *can* matter, but she knows which ones *usually* do. So, when the workers in this area go for break, she stays behind, scanning again, looking for little signs she's learned to look out for: the smell of dog treats means packaging is getting torn, scuff marks on labeled boxes means the labeler has vibrated itself out of alignment again, jumbled bins mean someone new is in replen. But since this is a new customer, she also breaks open a few completed boxes. This goes way beyond checking to see if each item is there. She wants to understand how the products will interact in the box. She takes each piece, holds it up to the light, drops it, and even smells it. Then she puts them all back in the box, shakes it around, and opens it back up. But she also zooms out from the box itself—looks at the space for breaking down inbound items—and checks the "rack and stack" storage available for excess output. She wants to understand the whole problem. Sita feels like a "detective" where each clue is progress in a race for productivity and quality. Part of the way she does this is absentmindedly puzzling about it all during her commute, or just sleeping on it. But she also knows that the fastest path to a win often requires keeping discoveries to herself for a while to see whether her team picks up on them themselves. When the group figures things out without her or with limited prompting, well, then she knows she's earned her pay.

Sita started out in a frontline, minimum-wage job in a warehouse just like this. She wanted a steady paycheck, so she did her task well: putting perfume samples in bags as they passed her on a line. Despite her dedication, if it wasn't for a nudge from Philip, her area supe, she might have stayed put. He noticed she was looking up and down the line more than most: "upstream" to the bag prep work and at the boxing station just a few people "downstream." So, without fanfare or explanation, he rotated her to boxing for a bit. He just said she should watch the taping. She felt like she was starting over, but she also learned a bit about how the taping machine worked—it applied a lot of pressure! Then Philip sent her back to the line. Now she understood it was important for bags to be evenly weighted to avoid crushing in the taping machine, so she gave them a light shake as they passed her by. A couple of weeks later he sent her over to prep work. All he said was "watch the product." That was enlightening: she saw how inbound pallets got broken down—where product got broken, lost, or stolen in the transfer to the bins, and how it got logged in the PC by the quality person. Then he sent her back to the line again, where she started telling her coworkers not to dig around in the bins—just take an item off the top to avoid breakage. Only after this deliberate, rich rotation through multiple areas of the work did he start asking her what problems she noticed. She thought there were too many starts and stops on the line. He agreed and told her to find out why. Two days later she came back and said it was that replen was slow with smaller items because they kept getting stuck in the bottom of the plastic product bins, and she showed him how. He promoted her to lead replen on the spot. She was dumbstruck—she hadn't even worked there yet—but she took it. From there on in, she kept up her detective work and tried to encourage others to do the same.

Sita displayed some remarkable qualities on her rise to management: motivation, attention to detail, and concern for the quality of tasks beyond her own. She kept enriching her view on the work, which put her on a fast track to building valuable new skills. What she did naturally is something that researchers have been trying to understand, and training and development leaders have been trying to replicate, for decades. How do you grow from a narrow skill set to a broader one, suited to a wider range of problems and circumstances? How do you engage with complexity: the uncertain, dynamic, and multidimensional aspects of the work? This means looking at the work through a wider lens, not a tight focus on a single task. If you're a dishwasher, for example, you might build a bit of understanding of plumbing and power. If you're a classical pianist, you might pay attention to recording technology or concert promotion. If you work in hotel housekeeping, you might look beyond your daily routine to the ebb and flow of seasonal rushes. Where challenge revolved around struggle to perform a task, complexity revolves around making sense of the context for that task. When you have healthy complexity, you understand more and more of the context for your work over time, and this lets you move from a narrow skill set to a broader one, suited to a wider range of problems and circumstances.

WE NEED HEALTHY COMPLEXITY TO LEARN

The traditions we drew on in the previous chapter—psychology, education, sociology, neurobiology, and artificial intelligence—offer strong support for the idea that we need healthy encounters with complexity for optimal skill development. Too much and we're overwhelmed. Too little and we can stop growing. In that sense, we're all like Sita.

Let's start with the fundamentals that cut across all the research: skill is your ability to get results in a complex world. When we start with no skill in a domain, we don't know how to handle the task, the goal, or the conditions for the work to be done. And we have to deal with a massive amount of complexity to even understand what a task is for, how it's performed well, and why that skilled performance gets results. In a now-classic study of field hockey, for example, Janet Starkes showed that expert players could "chunk and categorize" the game while they were playing in a way that allowed them to better direct their attention, predict events, and take effective action.[1] Instead of a bunch of separate moves, they could see a *play* and start one of their own to counter it. Or hear competitors' yelling as *poor offensive coordination* and substitute different defensive players to compensate. But for a total novice, dealing with complexity starts at the "what in the heck is even going on here" level: they need basic understanding so they can start to participate meaningfully. In the 1970s, John Anderson, a psychologist at Carnegie Mellon University, described this first step in tackling complexity as creating "declarative" knowledge: information you can write or say that is critical to directing your action but doesn't directly enable you to do the job.[2]

LET IMPLICIT LEARNING LEAD

Over the last thousand years, we have answered this "getting up to speed" problem with increasing formality: school, books, rules, checklists, and so on. These allow us time away from the action to get to know it intellectually. Obviously, codifying declarative knowledge has been incredibly helpful, allowing many more of us to prepare for the complexity of the world with much less help. And research shows that it's best to get this kind of knowledge shortly before we have to do the work itself.[3] The first time Sita showed up to a warehouse, she got a brief orientation, for example, where a line lead showed her the line she'd be working on, described what other workers did, and described the items the line produced. This was an efficient way to give Sita the information she needed to join the line. In the same way, she could enter the building because she got the same from her temporary staffing agency about what a warehouse even was. Experts know the basics, and they can help a lot by sharing them early.

But facts and rules only take us so far. In fact, if taken too far they can backfire. A great deal of research shows that if we rely too heavily on conceptual, declarative knowledge and rational thought to deal with the complexity that the real world presents, we can become *less* skillful.[4]

Let's start with swearing. Any parent who hears their child swear for the first time knows how much kids can learn just by observing. Albert Bandura, a Stanford psychologist, introduced social learning theory in the 1960s as he studied when and how kids learn to copy adults' poor behavior.[5] In an experiment that probably couldn't be done today for ethical reasons, he left children in a room with "bobo," an inflatable, egg-shaped creature about their size. In some cases, an adult stayed in the room with them, and played very aggressively with bobo first—hitting it, for example. In another room, kids were given a neutral adult model or were left to play with bobo alone. Perhaps unsurprisingly, the kids who had a model for aggressive play mimicked that when left alone—even though they never received any explicit instruction. Bandura and his colleagues thus gave us an initial peek at the idea that we learn just fine through watching, even without being taught. That is, at least, when we attend to relevant information—such as an adult's modeled behavior—retain it, and get a chance to use it. The novice baker learns to knead by following along with a master, move by move. The student learns Spanish far better by living with a family in Mexico. This way of learning has since been found in many other domains and it's gotten many names: implicit, vicarious, observational, incidental, and so on. This kind of learning is taking a particularly hard hit these days, given that we're deploying intelligent technologies in ways that separate novices from the action.

But the takeaway here is not just that implicit learning is important and effective. Explicit, declarative learning can actually get in the way. To see how, let's take a look at studies on motor skill acquisition.

Do you like watching pro tennis? Football? Gymnastics? Then you appreciate the wonder of a masterful athletic performance. Like Sita in her warehouse, athletes engage in graceful, effective action in messy, dynamic, intense conditions that most of us couldn't even interpret, let alone respond to. In most cases, those people had professional trainers, who studied the latest science on skill development. These experts would be well aware of research on "environmental regulatory features" (ERFs)—aspects of a context that matter for how we perform skilled action.[6] This research explores how we engage with complexity to build skill. It began when Antoinette Gentile, a leader in movement sciences and neuromotor research at Columbia, reset the global conversation on motor skills development by showing that the complexity of the task environment mattered for task performance. As she dealt with stroke rehabilitation patients, she noticed that the state of the art was to help them recover skills by training them with "perfect movements" in pristine, highly simplified environments. The working theory was that skill came from detailed, explicit instruction about the movement—making sense of the environment was an afterthought at best. Gentile noticed that patients struggled because their real-world conditions (for example, their breakfast table, bookshelf, or shower) were more chaotic. Gentile's insight—now replicated by performance coaches everywhere—was that technique wasn't as important as how the learner processed information about the task context.[7] We now know people learn best when they are put in realistic situations that are dynamic and interconnected—complex, not perfect. This is the difference between holding your hands in the right place over the keyboard versus typing at a reasonable clip in a loud café or a swaying sailboat. So she flipped the script, throwing rehab patients into plausibly normal task conditions after minimal practice, studying how they engaged with the environment as they tried to rebuild skill. Those patients did better.

Many other researchers have since focused on situational complexity. Experts in kinesiology, neuropsychology, physical education, and so on have found, for example, that implicit learning about a work environment—just getting in there and experiencing the complexity of a situation—is often better for skill development than significant explicit instruction.[8] Sita got "lucky" because she worked for a "hands-off" supervisor. After a brief orientation, she was put to work and received very little explicit guidance after that. Because she watched carefully and worked hard, a few months later she implicitly "knew" a lot about how the entire area functioned so she could "sub in" for almost anyone on the line. It was only after Philip noticed her and asked her how things worked on the line that she started to make some of this know-how explicit.

Sita's rich implicit training and Philip's timely, limited inquiry highlight the other core insight from psychological research on situational complexity: early on, explicit instruction should only serve to direct the novice's attention to "information-rich" (that is, complex) aspects of context without interpreting them.[9] Philip didn't tell Sita how everything worked, or how to do her new tasks as she rotated through new areas. He didn't even ask her to analyze what she was experiencing. All he did was suggest she focus somewhere new. He noticed that her natural inclination was to look at what other people were doing. So, in the boxing area he nudged her to look at technology. Then he noticed she treated "defects" (broken or missing product) as normal, so he encouraged her to "watch the product" as it came into the presort area. She learned implicitly once her attention was directed properly, so when it was time for Philip to ask her for potential process improvement, she had a wealth of skill to draw on. Now she does the same thing with her teams: minimal prompting to look at something, but not specifying *how* to look or *why*. As Richard Magill, a kinesiologist at New York University, says: "Don't ask [a trainee] how the ball was released, ask 'Where were you looking to see what type of pitch it was?'"[10] The first question asks a novice to examine a specific part of the action and to pick it apart. The second question just asks them where they were looking to understand the situation. Option two is better: once a learner's attention is directed properly, implicit learning is more effective, and should take over. The same "less is more" view is clear in the scaffolding research from the prior chapter. Learning this lesson is important because we have a lot of cultural and organizational conditioning that strongly suggests a more "micromanagey" alternative: specifying something for a novice to analyze or getting them to break down their technique. Telling a copywriter to break down how their company uses pronouns. Asking a glassblower to describe precisely how a master keeps glass molten. Telling a flight attendant to describe the most common techniques for resolving customer complaints. And that really gets in the way of novices' skill development. The skill code thrives in "goldilocks" territory: not too much complexity, not too little. Not too little direction or information, not too much.

NO REFLECTION, NO SKILL

So, you're in a complex learning environment, and you've got increasingly complex tasks and an expert pointing out where to pay attention. You're on a fast track to skill, right? Not quite. There's another critical component of how we come to terms with complexity: reflection. Research on learning and skill building agree on this point: you don't just build skill by *doing*. You need time away from the action to make sense of all the complexity you've dealt with. Here again, K. Anders Ericsson ignited elegant insights. Through study in domains ranging from taxi driving to chess to neurosurgery, he and his colleagues find that top performers form "increasingly sophisticated mental maps" of the work to be done, including environmental factors that could shape any surprises or contingencies they need to handle.[11] The richer the factual data they include, the better they are. His now-classic example here is of London cabbies, who begin by riding over three hundred common routes via bike, not only memorizing them but also implicitly learning about the range of conditions—like pedestrian traffic, weather, and even festivals—that affect navigation and the experience for a cab customer. But they don't build these mental maps during their rides—they do it during soak time before and after the actual navigational act. It's this interplay between doing and reflecting that transforms a novice into an expert.

Research shows us that this mental representation work—the task of tackling all this complexity down to an understanding that helps us act skillfully in the situation—mostly occurs after the work is over, when we get a chance to rest and reflect.[12] This is what Sita did on her commute. But sometimes we get this chance right in the flow of work, too. When we run into problems, surprises, or novelty, and we're lucky, we pause to puzzle through what's going on and how to move forward: Donald Schön, a philosopher at MIT, called this "reflection-in-action."[13] Studies suggest that this "luck" works best when we already have a good general grasp of the complexity of the situation. We are "chunking and categorizing" like pros and "get" what's going on—and then we get a small surprise. A new wrinkle. We turn a wrench, and a nut won't move. Huh. We speak in perfect grammar in a new language, but we're not understood. Weird. Then we can puzzle and figure it out while we're working.

So, the closer you are to being a novice, the less you should rely on reflection during the action. But whether it happens in the moment or after the action, a lot of this processing and reflection is unconscious or implicit—we are literally laying down new neural connections and giving them a chance to settle in. Regardless, after a little soak time, we can see patterns in the action that we couldn't before, and these new patterns allow us to at least see a way to act more skillfully the next time we try. In fact, Ericsson and others' work on expertise shows we do just this: away from the action—on the bus, in the shower, over dinner—we visualize our own performance in an idealized version of the situation, given our updated understanding.[14] And this visualization is in many ways indistinguishable to our brains from the real thing. So, in a very real sense we are getting free, simulated practice by doing this visualization and the research shows that when we do this intentionally, we get more skill out of our next real practice opportunity. And we also visualize the work to come—in other words, we plan by imagining vignettes. Without intention, these tend to be fragmentary and semi-deliberate, and likely have some positive effect for skill, but we only have studies on the deliberate mental rehearsal. There the skill benefits are clear. We take these mental representations and visualization of the complexity to our next work experience, rest, reflect, and visualize again, and the cycle repeats. When Ericsson started his work, this was a bit of a radical idea. No longer: now any pro athlete worth their salt takes mental rehearsal just as seriously as their physical practice. And while it does settle down as we build expertise, our mental representation of all that complexity is never done. Partly that's because the world is always changing. Just when we think we're an expert, some aspect of the task—whether it's social, technological, or material—changes, and we have an opportunity to update our representations.

We have to be careful with the results of reflection, though. First, if we cling too tightly to our new understanding, our skill and performance will suffer. Psychologists know this failure mode as "reinvestment"—consciously trying to control normally automatic, implicit responses by consciously working through explicit rules.[15] If you're a golfer, for example, you'll like a key study in this area by J. P. Maxwell and colleagues at the University of Birmingham:

when given three thousand chances to practice putting, people who were high "reinvestors" retained a longer list of ideas, rules, and guidelines about how to do the job, and they performed *worse*.[16] To add insult to injury, other athletes could tell: they were much more likely to label these high reinvestors as "chokers"—people who were overthinking things. The goal, then, is to limit the explicit rules, ideas, and distinctions you acquire for how to do something, and avoid trying to consciously apply them to control the mechanics of your technique. Instead, focus on—even visualize—the outcomes you want to achieve and count on the implicit learning that will come through reflection.

Reflection can also lead us astray—to a place where we *think* we understand the complexity of a situation, but we're dead wrong. I call this "snapshotting": where a novice takes experiences like a single site visit or one conversation as representative of an entire situation that, in fact, is much more complicated. For example, in the beginning of her warehousing work, Sita looked at her coworkers' speed to think about how fast her line could go. That was what she could readily see, and it seemed to make a difference. But Philip told her to watch the replen folks instead, because steady resupply was the real bottleneck. Sita had snapshotted the complexity of the situation. The research on ERFs backs this up, too: it finds that when the task environment becomes more complex in some new way, learners will struggle to build skills without any adaptation to the changed environment unless an expert points out the change.[17] We are highly susceptible to the overconfidence that comes from snapshotting. For example, Kayla Jordan, a psychologist at the University of Waikato in New Zealand, worked with colleagues to show that after watching a trivially informative video of someone landing a commercial airliner, a ridiculous number of people felt they could confidently do so—at least without dying.[18] Now that you can see this challenge, imagine how much worse it can get when we insert technology into the work that both separates that expert from a novice and gives that novice a steady stream of hyperconvincing literal snapshots of the situation they think they're dealing with. Another cupful of techno-gas on the skills bonfire.

Research on expertise and skill shows that experts can help with this reflection problem by refocusing a novice's attention if they get distracted or build inaccurate understandings of what's going on.[19] Sometimes this takes the form of open-ended questions about what they see; sometimes it's asking them to predict what will happen next. But the point is to spot-check how they think their task environment works, and why it works that way. This is exactly what Philip did with Sita after sending her through all those initial rotations. Then he nudged her toward using that knowledge to make a difference.

But there's another, counterintuitive way to confront this problem: forgetting. Whether it's through lack of practice or simple absent-mindedness, dozens of studies across domains as diverse as surgery, aviation, and professional sports show that we lose touch with practical know-how we once had. Normally, this is seen as a bad thing: we may be foggy where things used to be clear. But having to *rebuild* our model of that complexity gives us a second run at the experience, and we can implicitly learn new things about the work that we missed before. Forgetting came to the rescue for Sita: after becoming an area head, she forgot how to fold a subscription box from flat cardboard. When she did it again for a new customer, she realized she could get it done in only two moves instead of the customary five—if she just had a piece of smooth sheet metal nearby to brace against.

Experts have a different problem: they *fail* to reflect. This is the blindness that comes with the "seen one, seen 'em all" phenomenon: after a while, if you've got solid skill, it's all too easy to fit your mental models onto most any complexity to predict what's coming. A recent example here is in a study of radiologists by Trafton Drew and colleagues at Harvard.[20] These radiologists were asked to find cancerous nodules in twenty-four lung CT scans. The researchers inserted an image of a gorilla—forty-eight times the size of the average nodule—in the last scan, and 83 percent of the radiologists didn't see it, even though eye-tracking software showed most of them looked right at it! This blindness to surprises and novelty limits the expert's ability to build their skill further because they're missing new complexity, and the hyperrealistic, data-driven representations from AI-enabled systems can make it harder for experts to question the reality they're being presented with.

Beyond forgetting, a key remedy for this expert blindness problem comes from a familiar but surprising source: newbies. In one way, this book has treated the lack of skill as an obstacle to be overcome: start as a novice and get away from that as soon as possible. And while that's not wrong per se, you can also see in all the examples and studies throughout this book that novices arrive at the work pretty clueless about how to do things, why things are done that way, and what is even going on. Whether or not they recognize it consciously, experts rely on newbies' new eyes and *lack* of expertise to break the trance that skill can put us in. So, while on the surface, collaborating with novices slows the work down and leads to more mistakes, the precious upside is that their "silly" questions and "sloppy" work call fresh attention to the situation, which helps experts pay better attention to complexity. In fact in chapter 6 you'll see that, in my own research, I've found that a small group of experts are relying on novices specifically to build skill with new, disruptive technologies. They're a critical resource.

COMPLEXITY IS YOUR GROWTH OPPORTUNITY

The research above offers powerful findings, but a lot of it is focused on a person trying to do a simple task in a relatively stable environment, where there's a clear and repeatable recipe for measurable success in that task. That obscures a key reality: engaging with complexity is how we find the *next* skill we want to master. Skill is a journey of choice, and complexity provides the menu.

This is where the research on work, apprenticeship, and occupations kicks in. It shows us that by taming complexity in peripheral domains, we don't just build focal skill—we climb a skill tree, where you get more choice the more you climb. Just as Menelaos the apprentice sculptor met with different tradespeople in the morning and came to understand their work a bit better, studies show that to proceed in our journey from one skill to the next, we need to go beyond building a focused, single skill to get a sense as to how the whole problem hangs together—how rushing something over here slows something down over there. Or how other people's tasks intersect with ours.

Let's kick this off by returning to Sita. Looked at one way, her story was about building skill at her focal task: putting things in bags or boxes without errors, at least at the start. But very quickly, she had to contend with the broader complexity of her work environment, and this basically "forced" her to build more and new skill. New products surprised and slowed her down, so she started to watch replen to better anticipate change. To get better compensation, her line had to produce well, so she started noticing what her colleagues were doing: who was faster, who was slower, who made more mistakes, who made fewer. And she started to watch final boxing, taping, and labeling because sometimes she and her colleagues had to stop the line for backups on that end of things. Expanding her view was important for her to do *her* job well, but it also left her with know-how about how to make a *line* work well. As time went on, these new skills became less about how to do her *current* job well and more about how to do her *next* job well. She was pretraining for the line lead job she eventually got.

Studies of real work and of skill development at work show the same pattern. Julian Orr's ethnography of copier repair at Xerox shows that, after they got a handle on the basics, repair techs would gather and share "war stories" over coffee.[21] These were often about unusual heroism and resourcefulness that left customers satisfied and reduced the likelihood of recurrence. To do this, techs had to learn and tell stories about much more than technical know-how. They needed to learn about their supply chain, so they could stash useful parts in their trunk. They had to learn "social graces" to handle local users who loved their beat-up old copier so much they resisted getting a new one. They had to work out how to jerry-rig a wiring connection by tearing apart a transistor radio. Like Sita, they spidered out into multiple adjacent aspects of their experience, tamed that complexity, and that made them that much more skillful at their primary task. Their war stories encoded these lessons, which told novice techs that at some point they would need to cast their gaze outside the immediate problem to get better at solving it.

I've deeply examined thirty-one occupations in my research career and have read studies on dozens more. And when it comes to building skill, the pattern is often the same: you start at a distance as a novice, offering help and moving toward the "core" of the work as an expert decides you're ready. What's less well understood is that as you close in on that core—the most complex and difficult tasks available—in another sense you go broad: inevitably coming to terms with environmental dynamics that condition your specific task. The more you do this, the more you deepen your skill: you can handle surprises better, plan better, and help others see important but subtle patterns. And, like Sita, workers across multiple studies take this expanding negotiation of complexity as an opportunity to specialize in new skills. She realized, for example, that she was interested in what it took to keep "a good flow" of product through the building, so she built skill there. Another person might latch on to the mechanical side of things and end up in a maintenance job while another might realize they like the "computers" side of things and find their way into IT. Yet others realize they are "people people" and end up in human resources. By taming complexity in peripheral domains, you don't just build focal skill—you get access to the branches of an interconnected skills tree, and a clearer sense as to which ones you'd like to climb to next.

As with challenge, we find strong support for this approach in the fields of neurobiology and artificial intelligence research.

For the last few decades, neurobiologists have replicated this finding about the role "just-right" complexity plays related to visual recognition.[22] Basically, when primates—both human and nonhuman—are learning to recognize something new, it's best if there's some noise—let's call it complexity—in the visual field they're seeing. For instance, they might see a duck dive into the water in one instance, and then an albino duck, and then a normal duck but at a distance, then a female duck, and so on. This uncertainty invokes what neurologists call "recurrent processing"—a neurological phenomenon where your brain is essentially mulling over what it's seen, trying to separate the lesson from the mess.[23] When we get a healthy amount of recurrent processing—not too much, not too little—our accuracy, knowledge, and skill improve the best. Researchers have gone so far as to interrupt this activity—for example, by partially blocking our visual field when we're trying to classify an object—and have shown that when you block it, our learning gets interrupted, too. Our brains need complexity to grow.

It turns out that the latest artificial intelligence isn't quite the alien entity we all presume: it thrives with similar kinds of complexity, too. Similarly, developers of artificially intelligent systems—deep convolutional neural nets (ANNs, RNNs, or CNNs for short)—have found that noise-driven recurrence also helps their systems optimize their output. For example, just in 2021, Sushrut Thorat, Giacomo Aldegheri, and Tim Kietzmann showed that their object-categorizing RNN did better when they threw a bunch of apparently unrelated information at it, such as the object's location, orientation, and scale.[24] What difference do these things make for what kind of a thing the object is? Not much, you would think, to a human or a machine. But this "noise" improved their RNN's success. Here's a bit of juicy jargon from a key paper: "while auxiliary information is category-orthogonal and not category-diagnostic, it is extracted and used by recurrent networks to guide and improve performance." In other words, irrelevant noise can make the output better. But not too little, and not too much. Sound familiar?

Another link to complexity and machine learning has to do with a problem known as "overfitting." AI learns to predict patterns in data by training on a previous dataset: give it data labeled with outcomes you care about, then ask it to predict those outcomes in comparable data without the labels. Overfitting happens when your AI becomes superb, but your data itself is the problem—it's too limited, or perhaps too perfect, and when the system is set loose in the world, it needs perfectly consistent conditions to work. The solution to overfitting is to make things more challenging for AI, most notably through a technique that Nitish Srivastava and colleagues called "dropout."[25] Fiendishly simple in retrospect, their innovation was to randomly drop units and connections from their own neural network as it grew. In other words, they made the AI "forget" what it once knew to challenge it to learn again.

Remember GANs—the adversarial group of AIs that researchers set up to improve overall system learning? After a fashion, forgetting is actually the critical way learning happens there, too. When the generator and discriminator compete, it's the one who *loses* who learns. That model gets penalized by having its parameters significantly and semirandomly reworked: that's like having your memory partially wiped! Next round it might do far worse, but then again, maybe much better, because it gets a second chance to digest its task complexity.

FINDING COMPLEXITY IN YOUR ORGANIZATION, OCCUPATION, AND WORK

To protect healthy complexity, we have to be able to recognize it. This *sounds* deceptively simple: it's about widening your view to take in the whole scene, right? Not quite. As with a naïve definition of challenge, this would probably hurt skill development, because it's not fine-grained enough. To build skill while we work, we need to engage with complexity in the right amounts and in the right way. We've traversed quite a range of characteristics, so let's sum them up with another ten-point checklist. You're facing healthy complexity when:

- ❑ You learn basic facts about the work close to when you have to get started.

- ❑ You minimize up-front explicit learning—once you're oriented, it's usually better to learn implicitly by getting to work.

- ❑ You reserve explicit direction and instruction to direct attention toward complexity but avoid interpreting it.

- ❑ You have slack time to reflect on the work—away from it to start, during the action as you gain significant expertise.

- ❑ You reflect through visualization—imagining vignettes of action and consequence, and you envision alternatives.

- ❑ You don't try to control your automatic responses in the work by consciously thinking through rules.

- ❑ You get time enough away from the work to forget about some significant parts of it.

- ❑ You have an expert who asks about or redirects what you're paying attention to, but who limits telling you about what you're seeing or why it is the way it is.

- ❑ In return, experts treat your naïveté as an asset—encouraging "silly" questions and asking for your assessment before sharing theirs.

- ❑ The better you get at a task, the more you look into your broader work context, and pay more attention to parts of it that interest you.

Like most leaders, you probably don't know enough about how complexity appears throughout the organization, but you have the power to investigate this at scale, given that you can redirect your organization's resources. You can hire or redirect people to get a clearer picture, and to understand how things ended up as they are. For example, what processes degrade, prevent, or limit healthy complexity? Why? Does your orientation process, for example, overly restrict implicit encounters with complexity, or provide excessive explicit instruction? What about the role of new technologies in that situation? Through this kind of inquiry, a leader in a structural engineering firm might discover that time pressure or dynamism in her business drives engineers to digest complexity of new design approaches in ways that produce more skill. Or she might discover a workgroup that is boosting skill through its "notorious" rejection of procedure regarding contracts. Or maybe that new engineering hires get "thrown in the deep end" in ways that serve their learning. Beyond looking at your organization and how it runs, now you have another set of lenses to wear as you think through how you're investing in training. You will learn when it makes sense to focus your efforts—whether on specific areas, occupations, customer efforts, and so on—and when to make broader changes to organizational infrastructure. Getting a good assessment should be your main goal, regardless. And be sure to look in the mirror: you and your team face healthy complexity in some ways, not as much in others. Making a public study of this can be a powerful tool for improvement.

No leader just investigates: you should also invest in healthy complexity—for you, your team, your colleagues, and your organization. The first best investment is often stopping or dropping something, so finding the wise play can reduce cost. You will most likely find examples of "information bloat," for example, in theory provided to reduce uncertainty and save time. For a retail executive, this might be a monthly memo to store managers. For a manager in a spaghetti factory, this could be a group of manuals for onboarding. For a leader in a government agency this might be guidance provided through an on-site inspector. In cases like these, eliminating that memo, manual, or role can revive healthy complexity. Or you might eliminate or greatly reduce up-front training, reserving it for after workers have some implicit learning under their belt. And on the positive side, you can work the checklist for healthy complexity into your goal-setting and performance-review tools. Perhaps you could formalize after-action reviews that mandate reflection time. Or give managers feedback on how well they're doing on directing workers' attention with limited interpretation. As you well know, publicly rewarding success against a measured metric can lead to real change.

Are you on an occupational certification board? You have a different form of power when it comes to complexity. Do the norms and rules you set pose any threat to healthy complexity in your members' work? Are your policies for certification and training with new tools consistent with the requirements for healthy complexity? For example, a professional nursing association might create rules that limit the kinds of help that auditors, proctors, and mentors can offer as new nurses encounter complexity in their first year of clinical work, and at the same time they might mandate more structured rotation across clinical areas to enrich the scope of work that members have to face as they practice. They might also mandate "selective use" of technologies that overdeliver fine-grained data about nurse performance—for example to the wrong people at the wrong time. You might want to reconsider your policies and technologies if they don't accomplish comparable goals.

Whether you're the learner or the expert, you can use this checklist to identify what you need to change to improve outcomes for you and those trying to learn. Take an honest look at your work. Does it pass the healthy complexity checklist? For example, have you been exposed to a restricted set of experiences that has left you vulnerable to snapshotting? Was technology involved? For instance, a security guard responsible for a large facility might take a long, hard look at their information dashboard—real-time data from cameras, motion, weight and temperature sensors, and badge use—to figure out where implicit learning is helpful and where they could use a few pointers on what to pay attention to. Likewise, they might look for what parts of this information fire hose they find most interesting and spend some extra time with them. Finally, if you're the expert, take a look at how you're collaborating with those trying to learn. Do they face healthy complexity, and has that changed with the arrival of new technologies? To improve things, a journeyman plumber might try simply directing their apprentices' attention at a problem once they got set up at a job site, for example. Or a vocal coach might shift to asking his students to pay attention to tension and ease in their bodies before offering detailed instruction on muscle relaxation. And both can now consider whether recording and analyzing actual work performance is useful or harmful for novices' reflection.

No matter how far removed your life and work are from a warehouse, if you can deliver under pressure then in critical ways you and Sita are identical. Anyone with skill is. To get to the place where you could quickly understand a situation, know what to do, and then get it done, you needed healthy encounters with complexity. You had early, solid access to basic information. Someone helped orient you, but not too much. You had reasonable opportunity to reflect. You didn't overthink your work as you did it. And nearby experts treated your naïveté as an ephemeral asset, asking for your take and learning from it, knowing it would soon fade. Those things didn't have to happen, though, so you now better understand your good fortune when it comes to skill. In fact, as with challenge, you now have a checklist for complexity, so you're far better equipped to protect it—and the skill that follows.

We're not done with the skill code, however. If you think back on Andre's or Sita's story, you might see that challenge and complexity aren't the whole story. Yes, they both have to do with very different aspects of our working experience, involve very different ways of paying attention, practice, and interaction with the work environment. But they're also very much about the self, and the task. But we aren't robots and can't make the skills journey on our own—skill lives or dies because of our very human relationships. To get at this final, critical component, we're going to spend time with Emily.

CHAPTER FOUR

CONNECTION

I t took Emily six years to become a director of enterprise sales at her current company. She manages a team of enterprise sales executives (ESEs) who sell "software as a service" (SaaS) to help corporate clients manage huge construction projects like building skyscrapers, bridges, and highways. She wakes up early and starts her day with a cup of coffee and a quick scroll through emails on her phone. She replies to a message from Mike, an ESE with some pricing questions he needs to answer before he can ink a deal with a new client. Once Emily gets to the office, she puts her phone away so she and Brandon, a newer ESE on her team, can focus on a quarterly "pipeline review"—checking in about his current list of prospects and talking through ways they will move them forward. Brandon regards Emily as a role model and wants to impress her, so he took extra time preparing for their meeting. Today was tough, though: Emily told Brandon she was disappointed. Brandon made no mistakes, and his performance was good, but that, she explained, was her concern: he's not challenging his prospects enough. He's not pushing them to think bigger about what's possible and deprioritizing them if they won't. It isn't easy for him to hear—a jolt to his work world, really—but he agrees she's dead-on. Although he was reluctant to admit it, he had been frustrated with his deal size and sales velocity, and Emily's reasoning explains part of why he'd felt that way, but couldn't quite see it himself.

Emily asks Brandon if he wants pointers on how to shake things up. He says no—he wants to take a shot alone. Give me a couple of weeks, he says, to plan and execute a new approach. She tells him to go for it. Emily trusts and respects him, and she says so. He always steps up, listens carefully, and asks smart questions. And he knows that her door is open.

After the review, Emily heads to her floor's kitchen for her second cup of coffee. There she chats for a while with Nadine, a young sales development representative (SDR) who generates leads for ESEs to follow up on. Nadine's going to a Taylor Swift concert next week and Emily demands pictures, and they talk over favorite recent covers of Taylor's songs. Then Emily returns to her desk, coffee cup in hand, and scrolls through a system-generated report laying out her team's portfolio. She scans for surprises, whether it's stalled deals, new deals, or big potential prospects, and pays particular attention to "High Priority" or "Risk" flags for each sales campaign. She sends out a couple of emails and chats inquiring into these before heading to another conference room for a call with Anoosh, another ESE on her team. This meeting is with one of those high-priority, flagged opportunities: a Fortune 500 company they've never done business with. Over an agenda-free, relaxed lunch with Anoosh last week, Emily got some color on the deal: yes, Anoosh managed to get the meeting and knows the industry but has never dealt with anything so large and high-stakes as this particular opportunity.

Emily hangs back at the meeting. Anoosh proposes the agenda and runs the meeting, making a point to introduce Emily to the "economic buyer"—the person who will ultimately sign a check if they do business. Emily responds by suggesting a relationship-building dinner when she and Anoosh are in Bangalore in two months and says that she's glad Anoosh will be guiding the exploration of this opportunity in the meantime. The client warmly agrees, while she and Anoosh exchange a silent high-five. Emily excuses herself and Anoosh resumes the conversation with the client.

Emily builds her day, her task list, and her energy through relationships with clients and colleagues. Unlike earlier in her career, when she was focused on her own achievement, now her focus is on members of her team; their sustained success and satisfaction are what she's measured on and cares about, so she is laser-focused on building their capacity *and* relationships in each interaction. For her, that means while she nudges them toward less and less dependence on her for help, she works on getting to know them as people—what they enjoy, their habits and quirks—and sharing the same with them. She makes brief notes on it all, so she can keep this kind of communication going just as she's ensuring the team is excelling in the work itself. Maintaining relationships like this makes her feel good, but it also builds mutual respect and trust; they view Emily as an expert but also someone who cares. That's the legacy she wants to leave, and what makes her feel fulfilled. Today she got one unsolicited tip on a great potential new hire for exactly this reason.

Emily can put herself in the shoes of just about everyone on her team. She's been there, done that, having started as an SDR herself, cranking out leads as fast as she could. As an SDR she was assigned to work with three execs—Torsten, Anil, and Craig. While they were remote in their sales territories, Emily was working full-time at her desk in the Manhattan office sitting next to the other two SDRs. She learned a lot in that job, because her execs let her: when Emily was able to schedule high-quality calls for her colleagues, they would invite her to be a "fly on the wall" for the meeting. She said yes, every time. That way she could listen to how they built relationships, starting with intro calls all the way through purchase, ongoing use, and "cross-selling" to new opportunities at the same company. She'd ask her three bosses about it all afterward. They saw she cared, so they'd let her pitch in a bit. Building these skills helped Emily get her first sales executive job, but her hiring manager also told her that he had selected her because Torsten, Anil, and Craig all vouched for her. She's still in touch with those three guys today, but now they are peers. They bounce ideas and complex scenarios off each other and joke about the "good old days"—just six years ago—when Emily was a newbie.

No matter her position, Emily develops and relies on connection—bonds of trust and respect—to build her skills and help others do the same. She has formidable skill as a result: she's an ace negotiator, prospector, and deal maximizer. Her emphasis on relationships has put her team in the number one position in the firm for the last two years. We don't usually think of human relationships as having much to do with skill, but research from a variety of disciplines confirms that it's an essential component of the skill code: no connection, no skill.

WE NEED HEALTHY CONNECTION TO LEARN

We often celebrate leaders who received *The Devil Wears Prada*–style mentorship—isolation, lack of direction, harsh critique—but these are typically the harbinger of poor skills development. And all too often, we think of skills in individualistic, egocentric terms: all you need is a good head and nimble hands. That masks the fact that we simply can't get healthy challenge and complexity without healthy human connection. So, if challenge and complexity are more about the "how" of skill, this chapter is more about the "why"—more to do with a rich, complex, and very human landscape built on warm bonds of trust and respect. So say the fields of psychology, education, and management, but recent developments in neurobiology and artificial intelligence lend even more credence to the idea, too.

This has an externally focused aspect that's about practical opportunity: Want a chance to work at all, let alone get access to healthy challenge and complexity? Good luck getting it on your own. One or more people have the power to admit you to the party, let you stay, and lend support. But there's also a more internally oriented aspect that's about personal meaning: we get motivation for our work when it builds respect and trust with those who share our values. Let's start with questions of the heart, like "Do I feel connected?" or "Do I feel motivated to gain the respect and trust from those I aspire to become?" We often dismiss these as unconnected with hard-nosed skill and results, when in fact they're closer to the main event.

This became much clearer in the 1980s and '90s, when psychologists Edward Deci and John Ryan—who met at the University of Rochester—introduced self-determination theory, which has become one of the most influential, accurate, and useful theories in all social science.[1] Deci and Ryan helped us see that we aren't motivated to build competence in a vacuum. We fulfill it in concert with two other basic needs: autonomy and relatedness.

The idea that autonomy is a basic need is thousands of years old. You can find it in the *Tao de Ching*, the Vedic Sutras, and Plato. Early giants in psychoanalysis like Sigmund Freud and Carl Jung refreshed it near the turn of the twentieth century. The modern derivation came through decades of psychological research on people of all ages, many ethnicities and nationalities, at home, in the community, and at work, which also proved its impact: when we decide, on our own volition, to pursue a goal, we go after it with more energy than we otherwise would, and feel more fulfilled in life—even if the goal was someone else's idea.[2] This finding confirms a basic need to feel in control of our actions and goals, and to choose those that feel consistent with our sense of self. This is as basic as the need for competence. What's more, the needs for autonomy and competence are a powerful combination: when we get to choose our own goal and build the capability we need to achieve it, we get more motivation, creativity, and life fulfillment.

Emily knew and lived by this, intuitively. As she was finishing up her undergraduate degree, she decided she wanted to get into sales. It felt like a good match for her, so making the choice got her more excited. After scoping out all the different sales roles available, she settled on B2B SaaS in a larger organization—good pay and leading-edge, but stable. She knew she couldn't immediately handle the responsibility to sell large enterprise software contracts to Fortune 500 corporations, though. She needed to develop credibility, experience, and the selling skills necessary to be both qualified and successful. But she was fired up and this made practicing for her interviews feel like fun. She role-played in the shower, with her cat, and with her *very* patient boyfriend.

But if you asked her if she could have done it without other people, Emily would have looked at you like you had two heads. That's because she's also living proof of the third need at the core of self-determination theory: relatedness. This is the need for warmth, bonding, and care, which we meet by connecting with and feeling significant to others. Anywhere on the planet we look, as far back in time as we can see, we find evidence of humans trying to meet this need, and modern psychology shows us that when we get it met, our lives go better. Any time someone says we're "social animals," they're getting at the essence of this need. However introverted or extroverted you are, however you might act like you don't care for people, however differently you pursue human bonds, we are all alike in that we have a fundamental drive to build caring relationships with people and for them to hold us in high esteem.

SKILL IS SOCIAL

In 1972, MIT researcher John Van Maanen became a ride operator at the "happiest place on earth": Disneyland. Though he and his coworkers received forty hours of formal training (revealingly titled "Traditions I"), new recruits mostly learned how to interact with customers on rides through informal feedback and modeling the behavior of more experienced workers. This ran so deep that, by the end, customers were transformed into "guests," and rides became "attractions." This didn't happen because of Tinker Bell's fairy dust: seeing what more senior employees did and trying to fit in was the only way to become adept at performing a host of Disney-specific skills. Choice by choice, day by day, these new employees marinated in Disney's work routines, training, lingo, and informal interaction style, all infused with values and beliefs that reflected Disney's worldview. Van Maanen wrote up this transformative process in an article fittingly titled "The Smile Factory."[3]

This, right here, is how connection shapes our self-determined pursuit of skill. We are not born with an idea of what we choose to pursue and master—the specific competence targets we aim for. The only place we *can* get those goals and motivation is the people around us as we bond with them and seek their approval. Social scientists refer to this process as "socialization"—where an outsider (at the beginning, a new human) is introduced to a social experience and given a flood of reactions that suggest how one ought to behave in that situation.[4] The longer we willingly choose that relational environment, the more we internalize it all. This is true whether we become motorcycle mechanics, rocket scientists, actors, college professors, or book editors. Other people guide us and help shape our understanding of what's appropriate and inappropriate, valuable and not valuable, right and wrong, and so on. We don't always agree with them—in fact sometimes we decide not to pursue certain kinds of mastery because we find out we don't share and don't want to adopt the values of those who hold them. But even so, we are deciding what our next competence targets are in response to this drive to seek caring bonds and respect from other people. The strength of our connection with others shows us what skills we want to develop. In an age where our technologically mediated interactions are getting "thinner"—shorter and less substantial—this connection is taking a serious beating.

But connection doesn't just shape the direction of our growth in skill and competence—it motivates us to keep trying. As noted in previous chapters, immediate and direct feedback stimulates and sustains motivation: we tie a knot and it holds; we click the right box and get the screen we want; we make a stack of boxes that doesn't fall over. But research since the 1950s definitively shows that other people are almost always in the picture, and we get motivated when we hear from them. It's not just task feedback that motivates us— it's feedback from experts whom we admire and aspire to become.

Sociologist Douglas Harper recounted this important interplay between autonomy, feedback, and connection during his six-year apprenticeship to Willy, a mechanic and tinkerer in upstate New York.[5] At first, Willy taught Doug about iron, heat, basic welds, and tools. Seeking Willy's approval and respect for basic work motivated Doug to try harder and to get better. And Willy knew a little something about the power of this connection: he cleared the way for Doug to practice a new skill but didn't get overly prescriptive about how he should practice it. He intuitively understood that giving Doug some room to practice his new skills would motivate Doug to learn while getting the best help from him on the job at hand. In the language of self-determination theory, Willy attended to Doug's needs for autonomy and competence. This is the same pattern that shows up in dozens of studies: when we hear we're doing well from an expert, we're essentially learning that we've done something significant in their eyes, and this recognition plays a critical part in how we form relational bonds and, in turn, stay motivated to keep learning.

Connection works both ways. It's not just newbies looking upward. Experts, too, need warm bonds and respect. As so many of us know, the connection between mentors and mentees can be long-lasting and profound. In 1983, Kathy Kram, recently graduated with a PhD from Yale, published perhaps *the* foundational study on this very special bond. At a public utility with more than fifteen thousand employees, she did intensive biographical interviews with mentor-mentee pairs, spread across the different phases of that relationship.[6] The patterns she discovered reflected age-old understandings of how we navigate the phases of our life: as we enter the workforce, we are seeking a solid identity, role clarity, and a sense of connectedness. But once we are established as experts, we face a challenge around the meaning of it all—what psychologist Erik Erikson called "generativity vs. stagnation."[7] We seek opportunities to make our actions count toward something greater. So, while mentees in Kram's sample got a role model who accepted them, counseled them, and sometimes even became a friend, senior managers got their relatedness needs met, too. They built a warm, caring bond with a novice who looked up to them; they derived satisfaction from helping someone they saw as having "potential." Partially, senior managers' satisfaction came because they were ensuring their legacy, but senior managers also enjoyed respect from peers and superiors who viewed them as making a contribution to the next generation of promising talent in the organization. No matter how expert we become, we don't ever stop needing caring relationships and feeling that others see us as significant. We need to help and be helped, impress and be impressed. It's how we're wired.

Mentor-mentee relationships are a special, durable kind of expert-novice connection that can last for years. And they can go way beyond the bounds of work, extending into lifelong friendships long after any direct work collaboration winds down. Many expert-novice connections are far shorter, less involved, and don't promise such extensive life fulfillment. But that doesn't mean we can't learn about expert-novice relationships from mentor-mentee relationships. Both involve the same human needs. Mentor-mentee relationships are, in the lingo of social science, an "extreme case"—a great setting for research because certain dynamics appear more regularly and vividly. Once we use these cases to build a theory of how things work, we can then see how applicable that theory is—or isn't—to more subtle scenarios. In this case, we can ask whether mutual needs for relatedness animate shorter-lived expert-novice bonds, not just formal, relatively rare mentorships.

Emily knows they do. For every significant mentor she's had in her career—from Mrs. Wilmot, her tenth-grade English teacher who encouraged her to pursue a communications and business double major in college, all the way up to Torsten, Anil, and Craig at her first "real" job—Emily has worked with dozens of experts, and learned best when their collaboration was driven by warm bonds of trust and respect. Eddie, a senior SDR when Emily started, spent only a few extra hours tutoring her on Salesforce, the software her company used to track potential prospects. But he was kind, patient, and pushed her to get practical with the tool; he was a real lifesaver to her at that moment, and she'll never forget him. Likewise, she's been a "capital M" mentor to only a couple of people so far in her career, but she brings the same orientation to every interaction with people trying to learn. Take Nadine, for example— the SDR who's off to the Taylor Swift show. She's not a mentee. She doesn't even work for any of the ESRs whom Emily manages. But Emily takes satisfaction in getting to know her, supporting her journey, and feeling her admiration. Day by day, conversation by conversation, the respect and warmth in Emily's connections give her visceral evidence that she's on track in her development, and that she's doing the same for the novices who work with her. It's all getting harder, mind you, given a work-from-home, screens-and-keyboards, digital-everything world that we're building for ourselves. But she's crafty and determined, so she fights like hell to preserve her connections.

To put those technothreats aside, the research backs Emily up here. By the mid-1980s, studies driving self-determination theory had shown us that our most precious commodity was a combination of intrinsic motivation and life satisfaction.[8] Researchers started to ask what made a difference for these outcomes. The answer was stark and simple: no relatedness meant no motivation and meaning. Many of these studies were based in schools. For instance, Andrew Martin, an educational psychologist at the University of New South Wales, and colleagues surveyed 3,450 high school students on the quality of their relationships and checked these against their academic results.[9] It turned out that the quality of the student-teacher relationship predicted academic performance and satisfaction more than anything else. More recent research from the workplace tells the same story: the value and impact of quality relationships runs deeper than successful performance of the task at hand. In 2016, Amy Colbert, at the University of Iowa's Tippie College of Business, and two colleagues delivered watershed science on this matter.[10] Through a study of employees and their managers at a financial services firm, they showed powerful links between positive workplace relationships and employee "flourishing," which they defined as "experiencing positive emotions, finding meaning and purpose in life, and achieving one's potential." The follow-on work is clear: positive relationships are critical both to very personal matters of motivation, significance, and a sense of a life well lived, and to our evolving competence.

So, we know that if we don't get our relatedness needs met, we will lose motivation for our work, and it will mean less to us. The point of starting here is to recenter the conversation: literally thousands of studies show those are outcomes worth pursuing all for themselves. Full stop. The happy news is we've also gotten confirmation from recent research that there are rich and hard-edged links between these findings and skill: no healthy connection, no motivation and meaning; no motivation and meaning, no competence.

RELATIONSHIPS TAKE WORK

If we take a look across research in sociology, psychology, education, occupations, skill development, and even neuroscience, we can see a pattern: to get access to the work—the place where we can actually get the challenge and complexity we need to build skill—we need to earn the trust and respect of the experts involved. They then allow us to participate in a way that matches our ability. As we deliver results, we build skill, but we also earn more of their trust and respect, which are crucial for opening up the next opportunity. This is all animated through three tactics, every step of the way: attunement—paying close attention; feedback—sharing information about the relationship and seeking the same; and joint commitment—ensuring next steps meet both parties' needs.

Let's unpack this work, one aspect at a time.

Trust and respect sound simple enough: people trust us when they are willing to be vulnerable to our actions in risky situations because they expect we'll deliver. And people respect us when they are willing to give us valuable resources because they admire and hold us in some esteem.[11] But while simple in theory, we know from practical experience and a great deal of research that both are complicated in practice: hard to earn and easy to lose. And without them we don't get access to skill.

One of the first studies that showed this was presented in *Boys in White*, Howard S. Becker's 1961 book on medical residency.[12] After passing the gauntlet required to get into a residency, newly minted doctors expected access to the challenge and complexity they needed to learn—real patients, hard problems, serious risk. They were disappointed. Becoming a resident got them access to the periphery of the action—in the ballpark, but not on the field. To be assigned to interesting cases with high-quality supervision—in the language of this book, to get healthy challenge and complexity—they had to demonstrate good "comportment." Did senior docs think trainees interacted with patients, nurses, and staff in ways that befitted a resident? Did residents know their mentor's preferred approaches to certain medical problems, even when many approaches would do? If the answer to questions like these was "no," or "I'm not sure," the resident would see very little action. To help answer them, some residents—like successful novices in dozens of studies—took on scut work that experts would see. These are small, early ways for an expert to assess how motivated and capable a novice is—of fitting in, coordinating well with others, doing things the way the expert thinks they should be done, and so on. The result? Trust and respect: the tickets to *play* in the ball game (or the operating theater or emergency room, in this case). I saw exactly the same thing across the four studies I've run in surgical settings, and this dynamic is evident in most any study of occupational progression.

Emily knows there's a dark side of earning trust and respect by fitting in, however. In her first sit-down with Anil, he told her something perplexing: "Do just what we tell you, and get along with everyone, and you'll be out of a job in six months." What did he mean? He and other experts trusted and respected novices who *cared* about contributing, getting better, and treating the people around them well. They hoped novices would positively defy expectations. This often looked like going the extra mile—doing more and better than Emily was asked to do. For Anil—and many experts—showing expectation-defying initiative is an important part of the good comportment that earns trust and respect. In that kind of a world, following rules and meeting quotas can be a recipe for skills stagnation. Showing commitment isn't as easy as overdelivering, however. You have to show you care in a way that's consistent with local experts' values. The sociologist Michael Burawoy discovered this the hard way when he took a job as a machine operator in a Chicago machine shop in the 1970s. He wanted the machinists' trust and respect so he could learn from them.[13] So he joined an informal group of experts who played a game they called "making out," which involved producing more than their quota, but hiding that output from management. He worked extra hard and his coworkers quickly confronted him, saying he would make them look bad. It turns out their game was much more complicated than he assumed: it was about quality, safety, and solidarity among workers, too. The real informal rule? You don't race ahead unless the group does it together, strategically. The overall lesson links right back to socialization: we only rarely get told the standards for comportment and skill, and they can sometimes be in tension with each other, with some mattering more than others.

Of course, you can't earn trust and respect just by acting the part. You have to *do*, and do *well* in the eyes of those who have the authority to get you in the game. However intuitive and obvious this may sound, it was only verified scientifically about twenty-five years ago. Holly Brower, a research professor at Wake Forest University, and three colleagues published a particularly convincing piece of research on this in 2009, exploring the consequences for subordinates of trusting and being trusted by managers.[14] They surveyed employees and their managers across eight locations for a hotel and resort company, and found that as subordinates performed their tasks well, managers trusted them more. What's more, trusted workers contributed more to the health of the organization and were less likely to leave. But there's an important twist here, just as there was in the comportment department: studies have shown that when experts *have* more skill, they trust novices more. Jennifer Kogan, a professor of medicine at the University of Pennsylvania, coauthored two key studies here. First, she and her colleagues were left scratching their heads once they found that more expert doctors trusted medical students more.[15] To explain that, they did a qualitative interview study, and found that supervisors with less experience were less confident, so stuck more tightly to rules-based assessment of detail.[16] It's easier to see failures and inadequacy that way, so they anchored on those more than they should have, and trusted novices less.

Seeking trust and respect is what motivates us and getting them can earn us the opportunity to take our skill to greater heights. But knowing these are meaningful and necessary for skill doesn't tell us how to build them. This takes tactics—specific behaviors that enable trust and respect in everyday interaction. Let's turn to these now.

Emily knows these tactics like the back of her hand, and you can see the evidence peppered throughout your introduction to her. In fact, you can see her know-how in action just by looking at her pipeline review with Brandon. It was time for her to interact with him about a complex problem, so she made sure she was *there*: down went the phone; she looked him in the eyes and listened. When she saw his issue with growing his deal size—something she thought was ineffective and that she was disappointed about— she shot him straight about it. Then she asked if he wanted input on a solution. When he said no and offered a cogent plan, she said she trusted him. All this improved her respect for him, his for her, and their trust in each other.

Even if it was by intuition, in her review with Brandon and in her work in general, Emily relied on three tactics that are at the beating heart of the healthy connection: being attuned, giving feedback on the relationship, and joint adjustment. Let's examine these one at a time, starting with attunement.

We're attuned when we focus directly and entirely on someone and their circumstances—just taking it in with low judgment. This is critical because experts and novices both need good information about each other's task-related behavior, but also need to know that their counterpart cares. Emily knew this, intuitively, at that first critical sales meeting in her day: she put down her phone to avoid distracting herself, and to send a signal that she valued what was going on. Research showing the power of attunement for learning comes from various quarters—we have great studies on the power of "heedful interrelating" for learning in work groups, for example[17]—but the recent neuroscience on interbrain neural synchrony (IBS) is perhaps the most magical.[18] It has found that during meaningful social interaction—when we really attend to each other and feel more connected, engaged, and cooperative—our brains actually get "in phase" with each other, operating to the beat of the same electrochemical drum. We're starting to get studies linking this to learning: Yafeng Pan, a neuroscientist at East Normal

University in Shanghai, and colleagues found that when a teacher and a learner interacted more, their IBS was stronger, and the student learned more, too.[19]

When it comes to healthy connection, the story on feedback is refreshingly simple: we need to know how we stand in the relationship, not just how we're performing on task. Specifically, this means experts and novices communicate clearly and regularly about the status of care, trust, and respect between them. Remember, these are the aspects of our need for relationality, so this is what people will naturally be wanting to know about. This wasn't only evident in Emily's pipeline review with Brandon—she has always prioritized feedback about the relationship. When she was an SDR, she always gratefully accepted Torsten, Anil, and Craig's invitations to join sales calls, and asked questions that showed she valued their support, for example. As a sales director, she chats with her team members about their lives and interests, like she did with Nadine about Taylor Swift. And whenever she hears about a particularly enterprising or creative SDR, she carves time out of her schedule to show up, watch, and offer support, even though they're two or three levels below her in the organization. It didn't matter that a lot of that feedback was nonverbal—it was "just" a not-so-simple matter of showing up, sometimes. What mattered was that folks got the message. Yet again, the research is in Emily's corner: when we get clear information (feedback) that our bonds are warm and that respect is strong, we learn better. In 1997, Jason Teven and his advisor James McCroskey at the University of West Virginia found a very simple connection: students who felt their teacher cared for them also reported learning more.[20]

Like most things, positivity can be overdone—numerous studies in a range of disciplines have found that trust and respect improve when we feel we're getting and giving timely, accurate feedback that holds us accountable in a fair way. This applies just as much to the relationship as the task, so withholding concerns about the relationship can have a subtle, caustic effect on skill. You don't need to go beyond the confines of the last few paragraphs to see why: if you begin to have concerns about someone's trustworthiness or lose respect for them—or they feel the same about you—pretty soon the high-quality learning opportunities are going to get handed out to someone else. So, as with feedback more generally, the best path is to express negative assessments as soon as possible. We can see this in research on psychological safety by Amy Edmondson, from Harvard Business School.[21] She and her colleagues have found that in top-performing teams, members express disapproval about task performance or the relationship just like Emily did to Brandon: point to a gap and ask if you're missing something. The "trick" here is that you have to be genuinely open to the possibility that you don't have the complete picture or are even flat wrong. If you've got that mindset, then your question will be genuine. A pro forma inquiry won't cut it in matters of the heart. Beyond seeking for accurate, timely feedback on the relationship, another key remedy for novices is working with multiple experts. Kathy Kram's later work shows that novices do much better when they attach to more than one expert, for example.[22] But to step away from specifics, the research shows that warm bonds and mutual esteem need active, separate attention if we want the kind of connection that helps to build our skill. Find tactics that deliver that outcome and you'll be on solid ground.

If we take research on self-determination theory seriously, joint adjustment—trying for next steps that address both parties' needs—is a straightforward story, too. Both experts and novices have a need for autonomy, and their trust and respect for each other will improve when they allow each other to get that need met. After a bit of experience, Emily wanted to learn about the international side of the business, so Anil gave her some overseas prospecting tasks. For her part, Emily learned that he didn't really go for a lot of verbal feedback and debriefing after sales calls, so she toned down her more verbal style and learned to write up her questions. Joint adjustment doesn't mean everything's up for negotiation:

remember, the key for getting our needs for autonomy met is that we feel that our choices are our own, that they are consistent with our sense of self. So experts can and should typically still direct the work, set goals, and offer feedback—it's just they should also be attuned to how they might switch things up to allow novices satisfying authorship for their work and skills journey. This finding is evident in a range of research traditions in this chapter so far, but it is also core to the scaffolding research in chapter 2. Sometimes this adjustment can be in the form of an explicit, out-loud conversation about novices' goals and preferences. But other times—perhaps far more often—it's simply about tweaking work assignments to match novices' demonstrated capability and interest.

As we engage in these tactics—and build warm bonds of trust and respect—they start to become more externally focused. After some solid performance on task, a novice isn't quite a novice anymore. They've built real, differentiated skill, and have new, more complex skill goals. New novices may have arrived. This transition is where teaching, sponsorship, and, ultimately, "breaking up" and "paying it forward" come in as part of healthy connection.

Before advanced radar and digital computers, a battleship stayed on course because entry-level seamen stood at the edges of the deck and used an optical instrument called an alidade to take regular distance measurements to the shore. They called in their measurements to a bearing recorder—a petty officer—who plotted them on a chart in a windowless room. The recorder then called *their* work in to a "plotter" who used it to double-check output from a mechanical computer, and so on up the chain to the officer on deck, who issued control commands. Ed Hutchins gave us a book-length, boots-on-the-ground study of how this all got done.[23] He showed that you worked your way up this chain by doing your job well, but also by coaching the next most *junior* person down the chain while you worked together. If you were a petty officer, the plotter trusted and respected you not just because you gave good figures quickly, but because you were training the person doing the job you used to do. Yes, that's part of how you ensured you got good input, but it was part of the "pay it forward" ethos of most workplaces: you got help before; now it's time to show you can and want to help the next person coming up underneath you.

That's how breakups are part of healthy connection. When there's a warm bond of trust and respect between expert and novice, the novice builds differentiated skill in areas of the work that mean the most to them. As they do that, the expert will crow about them to others and expose them to alternative work opportunities. Then . . . they take them! What was once a hierarchical relationship transforms into a peer one. This was Emily's story: after a particularly big win on a sales call that she helped orchestrate, Craig introduced her to Bert, her next boss. But Bert already knew from the agenda that Emily had dug up the initial lead, and Craig made a point before hanging up with the client to thank Emily for making the connection. Instant hire. This pattern meets everyone's needs for relationality: we feel grateful and respect the expert more for supporting our development, and they feel more bonded to us and earn the respect of their peers for doing such a good job developing talent. And, practically, this almost becomes necessary if we're going to continue our journey to skill. Often the next healthy encounter with complexity will be outside our work area and away from that expert, so we rely on them for exposure and a public vote of confidence to get access to it. This is just how it went with Emily, Torsten, Anil, and Craig. When she got started with Bert, she still came to them occasionally for advice, but now they consult each other on problems and highlight their favorite novices to each other. They're more friends than anything else. Studies underscore this dynamic across a dizzying range of occupations in many industries: from film production[24] to automotive design,[25] open-source software[26] to craft bourbon production,[27] investment banking[28] to midwifery.[29]

But it is important to say that some experts and organizations are terrible at expert-novice breakup. In fact, they specialize in the opposite: talent capture. You can see this in an ethnographic study across all the big six accounting firms by Mark Covaleski and three colleagues at the University of Wisconsin–Madison's business school.[30] They found a troubling landscape of limited human potential: accountants everywhere were beholden to those above them, and production pressures inside their hyperspecialized domain meant they rarely got the chance to build extracurricular connections, skills, and opportunities. They suffered mightily for it: autonomy was built into their professional identity, and that ran in direct conflict with these managerial fiefdoms. They ended up feeling like "corporate clones" or alternatively engaging in subtle resistance that caused them a great deal of stress and loss of status. Protégés were even worse off, getting all kinds of mixed messages about toeing the line and resisting corporate "bullshit." The net effect was they were practically trapped in a near-unwinnable race to the top of their firm that required sacrificing their professional sense of self. We have similarly rigorous studies showing the same in education and medicine; domain expertise is hoarded, and silos of skill are protected. Talent capture is entirely unnecessary, of course. Even if we specialize as we build increasing skill, and even if we do this in large, hierarchical organizations, we can always take and make some time for self-directed skill development, whether we're the novice or the expert. We'll do better, build more skill, and be more fulfilled in our work the more we build connections that allow for everyone to meet the same basic needs: autonomy, competence, and relationality.

Healthy connection revolves around meaningful bonds of trust and respect that are about as human as it gets. So, it's really quite something that the very latest AI—technology that we often think of as alien, different, even superhuman—needs healthy connection to learn, too. This should give you a bit of hope and curiosity, given the technothreats I explore in the next chapter.

First, a single modern AI often has experts and novices built into it. A great example comes from Marcin Andrychowicz—a researcher at Google's Deep Mind—and colleagues at Oxford and the Canadian Institute for Advanced Research.[31] Before their work, a primary algorithm worked to accurately classify something—say a picture of a nerve cell. What kind? But expert humans were needed to hand-tune the algorithm's search for the best possible classification; otherwise it would take far too long. They made the ingenious leap of building a "meta-learner"—itself also a machine-learning model— that tried to model an effective learning function for the primary algorithm and nudge it into a shorter, more effective learning path. This worked, and dramatically reduced the training time for the primary algorithm. So, it's a pretty clear example of how AI functions better when it relies on healthy, almost social connections. This even extends to something like socialization across the human-AI divide. Paul Christiano and other colleagues from Google Brain, Deep Mind, and OpenAI in fact built a system with *three* actors: a primary AI, a meta-learner, and a human.[32] There the system asks a human expert to compare videos of the primary AI's behavior (say, navigating a virtual obstacle course), then enter which they prefer. That then trains the meta-learner, which gets better at predicting what a human would prefer. In many cases this produced desirable behavior *far* faster than a system could without human help, even when that human help was noisy and inconsistent. If you're seeing connections between this and the process that new Disney workers went through, as they learned to think and act like a member of the "smile factory," you're onto something.

FINDING HEALTHY CONNECTION IN YOUR ORGANIZATION, OCCUPATION, AND WORK

One of the curious characteristics of healthy connection is how obvious and intuitive it feels when it's happening. Perhaps it's best known by its absence. But as with challenge and complexity, here's a ten-point checklist to help you diagnose healthy connection, whether you are the novice or the expert. Digest it carefully; otherwise your journey to skill might be fatally flawed, and you might not know it. A connection is healthy for your skill when it:

- ❑ Provides warmth, bonding, and care.
- ❑ Gives both of you a sense that you and your work are significant in others' eyes.
- ❑ Builds trust: the other person's willingness to be vulnerable to your actions because they expect you'll deliver.
- ❑ Builds respect: the other person's willingness to give you valuable resources because they admire and hold you in esteem.
- ❑ Involves both of you being carefully attuned to each other, limiting distractions and judgments.
- ❑ Gives both of you feedback on how the relationship is going.
- ❑ Involves joint adjustment of goals, methods, and work assignments to allow both of you satisfying authorship of your work and skills journey.
- ❑ Eventually allows you to coach and teach others as you reach solid skill yourself.
- ❑ Eventually results in the expert advocating for you outside your shared project.
- ❑ Results in a "breakup" when you've built enough skill to handle complex projects mostly on your own.

With this checklist in hand, ask yourself what's working in your relationship with others, with your direct reports, your peers, and your boss, as well as in your organization and your profession. How can you be more attentive in creating this dynamic? Are there formal systems and structures that would help you and your organization lean into connection with more force and with better results? And how could you share this knowledge with others in a way that helps them do the same? For a third and final time, you're looking at a "meta" skill set: in this case the tactics required for cultivating healthy connection. The better you get at these, the more effective you'll be at fostering human bonds that build and sustain skill. And to pull a "double" meta, these checklists themselves show you what you need to do to cultivate this skill set for cultivating skill.

If you're a leader, ask yourself: Do you have good information about the health of the connections in your organization? If not, what are the riskiest gaps in your understanding, and how could you reallocate resources to plug them? Perhaps you're in an organization that relies on talent capture. You have an opportunity to unleash a tidal wave of human potential by breaking that cycle. Another key question: Where are healthy connections thriving in your organization, and why? A manager at an auto body shop might find out that restocking mechanics' kits—apparently low-value busywork—actually allows newbies precious face time with senior mechanics without disrupting the flow of work, for example. Or a legal executive might find their internal client management process includes some variant of joint adjustment, based on discovery of individuals' goals and interests. And you have huge questions when it comes to your training spend. How much does your learning and development architecture presume away the necessity for healthy connections—does it treat warmth, bonding, and caring as unrelated to skill building that comes from consuming online content, for example? In some areas of your organization, healthy connections will add more value than in others, so you should make targeted investments there. And in other ways, it's important that you find healthy connections wherever you go in your firm. But as with the other two Cs, your primary goal should be to get good data on connection, so that you can make good decisions. This includes you and your team: How do you fare on the checklist above?

Your job as a leader is to set a vision and mobilize for positive change. So, you should also invest in healthy connections—for you, your team, your colleagues, and your organization. As I mentioned in the previous chapter, our prior investments—in things such as rules and processes, roles, technical infrastructure, and perhaps even entire functions—can be an obstacle to skill. Stopping or dropping these can both save cost and unleash healthier connection. You might find professionals mediating expert-novice relationships in areas like recruiting, onboarding, training, and performance management, for example. How might you cut these intermediaries out to allow healthier connections to flourish? You can also set a positive vision here, checklist in hand: How might you measure and reward the behaviors associated with healthy connection, no matter the process or work area? We get what we measure, and most likely you need more care, trust, and respect between experts and novices to build the skills your organization needs to thrive.

Do you have decision-making power about the standards of your occupation or profession? The health of skill-enhancing connections is in your hands in a different way. Those standards involve norms and rules. Are they in some way related to threats to healthy connection showing up in your members' work? And how do your certification policies and training with new tools relate to that checklist for healthy connection? There are numerous certifications in software development. A leader on one of these boards—say for the Agile software development methodology—could look through their coursework, procedures, and guidelines to see if they help or hurt healthy connection. They might redesign the training for facilitating a scrum (a progress update meeting), for example, so that practitioners get nudged in healthy directions: toward attunement in their work with each other. Toward relational, and not just task feedback. Into interactions that will allow novices to demonstrate not just the hard skills they need to contribute to the codebase, but the professional demeanor that will earn the trust and respect of their expert collaborators. Last and probably not least, what about the role of new technologies—as a boost or drain on healthy connection? An executive for pharma-ceutical research and development might find that new data an-alytics tools and micro-experimentation rigs allow professionals to do more discovery work, but are also "distracting" them with work-related information when it would be better for them to be bonding as people.

Now let's say you're the learner—or the expert. If the question is how you can build your own skill or help someone else do the same, this list is a guide in the "soft" territory that many will treat as irrelevant to competence. Consider your job with a little relaxed distance. What it's like to inhabit it. Or what it might be like to be that novice, coming up the ranks. Is there enough humanity there? Enough healthy connection? Or maybe too much? The head of a facility's custodial staff might have developed bonds that make timely critique among janitors too uncomfortable, for example. Or a mill operator might realize that with a new, internet-connected CNC machine, she's got all the resources she needs to do her jobs without consulting much with senior technicians. Good for meet-ing her quotas in the short run, but if she wants one of them to vouch for her or back her up on a job, she might fall short. And that brings up the constant refrain in this book: technology often plays a role in healthy connection, for good and for ill. You'd best look into that possibility.

If you have expertise that you can rely on for results, it doesn't matter that you've never done B2B SaaS sales, and don't like Taylor Swift: you and Emily share the same experience. Just like everyone else with skill. To earn the trust and respect of experts, to perform on the job, and to get them to vouch for you for your next opportu-nity, you had to have healthy connections. They made you confident you chose your course yourself, that you were getting better, and gave you a sense of belonging and significance you needed for the journey. You showed good comportment and tactical skill; an expert recognized and approved of that, and gave you another shot. Maybe they became a mentor, maybe they didn't, but you connected with each other as people. You were attuned to each other, gave straight feedback even when it was uncomfortable, jointly adjusted the arrangement so both of you could feel more satisfied authors of your skills journey. And eventually, you started to coach people more novice than you, while the expert in the picture started to vouch for you in broader and broader circles. All that was optional. You're lucky when it came to skill. But now you have a much finer-grained picture as to why. That's empowering: you can use the checklist above to protect healthy connection for yourself and those you care about. And they might just trust and respect you for it.

If this book ended here, you would have a huge leg up in your journey toward valuable skill—either as an expert or a novice. But you read chapter 1, so you remember: chapters 2, 3, and 4 do not give you everything they need to preserve and enhance skill forevermore. Massive, exponential changes are crackling through the global economy and they're tilting the playing field in ways that make this catch-up game unsustainable. From videoconferencing to ChatGPT to robots and everything in between, we're handling our most advanced tools in ways that subtly but deeply weaken challenge, complexity, and connection. This will send our ability to build new skill down the drain if we let it run its course. So it's time to face this threat.

CHAPTER FIVE

THE THREAT

Like many companies, Emily's firm went entirely virtual during the height of the pandemic. Since its founding it had been an office-based culture, with sales reps and solution engineers traveling to meet potential and current customers. Despite that, the transition wasn't a total shock for Emily, her team, and teams like them: they were used to spending lots of time on the phone and videoconferencing, they dealt with all essential information via software-and-screens interfaces, and their persuasive work was already intangible. So, sending everyone home was stressful, but it seemed feasible and was obviously the right thing to do.

Right away, Emily—everyone—was concerned about the quality of customer relationships, and therefore deal size and velocity. Their concerns went something like this: if we couldn't spend face-to-face time with our customers, if we couldn't break bread and share a drink, how would we build the trust we need to sell solutions that leveraged the best of what our firm has to offer? Emily's direction to everyone was to double down: schedule more, shorter calls, send more tangible materials, and in general find ways to keep conversations moving. Meanwhile she got acquainted with all the videoconferencing, instant messaging, and collaboration platforms out there so she could make it easier for her reps to interact with their customers. She dug in further, meeting regularly with her IT rep, attending virtual conferences on virtual sales, and chatting with other sales directors dealing with similar challenges; indeed, she was becoming a bit of a geek.

She ran an excellent team, and they stepped up to meet these new challenges. For years now, she knew that even if she failed to show up on any given day, they would know what to do. So that's what they did: when she was at home in her pajamas tabbing through her sales dashboard or on the phone with her IT consultant, her ESEs took up the slack; they structured deals and managed their pipelines almost independently. Their SDRs kept the deals flowing, too—they sent collateral, hacked together new digital assets. And so on, down the line. Emily didn't tell them she'd be setting aside time and attention to deal with the challenge of the shift to virtual—and eventually hybrid—work, but they trusted her, and soldiered on. It took a few months and a brave SDR speaking up to let Emily know that, despite her good intentions, all was not good.

Fortunately for Emily, her wake-up call came after a particularly great deal closed via Zoom. Emily and her team were exchanging high-five emojis when she got a private text from Nadine, the SDR she used to chat with in the break room: "The team is dying. We're losing our edge." Emily messaged right back, asking for a one-on-one. They talked for an hour, and Nadine helped her see: by shifting to virtual sales and leaning into this new technology to expand her positive impact on the performance of the business, Emily was reducing her positive impact on the human bonds that allowed people to maintain motivation, build skill, and work their way up the chain. Fewer accidental collisions meant she was exposing her direct reports to less of her more strategic work, and the same effect ran down the line: profound losses in the challenge and complexity department. Everyone focused on their own, local problems, which meant folks had less opportunity to help each other and to experience each other's work. Big, missed opportunities for connection and complexity. None of these insults to the skill code was extreme or all that obvious, but on a day-in, day-out basis, they added up. The team was running to stand still.

Billions of us are headed toward Emily's scenario, and we need all hands on deck to set things right. We can see this better by looking at new technologies—they often intensify problems and solutions. Or as many believe the science fiction writer William Gibson put it, "The future is already here—it's just not evenly distributed."[1]

This is why I focused my early research on surgical work involving perhaps the most sophisticated robotic technology yet deployed in modern medicine.[2] This was deliberate: I wanted to look into our shared future, and one great way to do that is to study early adopters of advanced technology. We invented time zones to manage railroads, and this revealed how we eventually would deal with scheduling and planning throughout the economy. We created the technician role to deal with massive industrial-grade equipment, and understanding this showed us what to expect from technicians everywhere.

By now you know the result of my glance forward in time; you saw it with surgical resident Kristen in chapter 1. In 2014, she became a bystander while the expert surgeon did the whole job. Right away, I got curious: Was this happening beyond robotic surgery? On the surface, it was hard to fathom: this was hyperspecialized, life-or-death work involving extremely expensive and complicated technology, multiple professions, and a highly regimented environment. Not exactly representative of the wild world of work. So, I spent a year and a half getting deeply familiar with top-notch field research on radically different kinds of work and occupations, dealing with very different kinds of technology. After examining more than thirty-one occupations now—from law to music composition to food service—it's clear this isn't just about super-advanced, intelligent technology like ChatGPT or humanoid robots. In our quest for productivity, we're using new technologies in ways that make novices more and more optional in experts' work. That compromises healthy challenge, complexity, and connection—no matter who you are or what occupation you're in.

Over the course of the next several years, I did more of my own research and worked with a growing number of field researchers who were doing boots-on-the-ground studies of work involving other intelligent technologies—in diverse settings such as internet startups, policing organizations, investment banking, and online education. Like me, they spent hundreds of hours observing, interviewing, and often working alongside the people they studied—people who were making the transition from apprenticeship with a human to a world of learning alongside intelligent technologies. I reached out to researchers to get coverage across two important categories: intelligent technology as a tool to *do* the work and as the platform *for* the work. In microchip design, for example, engineers literally can't lay out a new design without using AI. Self-driving telepresence robots in eldercare, on the other hand, gave doctors a new way to "be there," but they still interacted with residents using the same skills they always did. Put together, our rich data showed the same dynamics I found in surgery. Across industries, technologies, occupations, geographies, and kinds of work, *See one, do one, teach one* was becoming *See one, and if-you're-lucky do one, and not-on-your-life teach one.*

Why? New tools such as machine learning, sensors, robotics, and cloud computing allow us an unprecedented ability to reconfigure jobs in search of improved results. This has many potential benefits, but one of the main ones is to help extend and scale the value of a single expert's skill. Let's step through an example in chip design. A design engineer can run an AI-driven algorithm overnight that searches through many potential configurations for a microchip. You can think of this problem as one of those "fit the blocks in the square" puzzles: a bunch of components need to be fit together—some to do with power transfer, some to do with computation, some that deal with signals between blocks, and so on. Tiny changes mean better performance—on power consumption, data retention, heat management . . . There's a long list, and moving a block to improve things on one dimension can make things worse on three others. Without the AI-enabled software, optimizing all these requirements could take a superb human engineer five to six days, and there are more opportunities for mistakes. And with that AI-produced output, that engineer can then rely on their subtle design sense and experience to make an intuitive assessment as to whether the software has spit out a solution that isn't creative enough. The expert makes better use of their highest talent, and speed and quality both improve. Everyone wins there, right? Wrong. You know who loses by now: the junior engineer—and, by extension, the organization and the entire engineering profession, which are hobbling the next generation of talent.

Before that AI-enabled tool came around, senior design engineers relied more heavily on junior engineers to run the simpler portions of the analysis required to inform the chip design process. The senior engineers would help them prepare for that analysis and examine the output, giving feedback all along the way. Junior engineers asked questions during this process so they could improve their work. Sound like a familiar process? One we've seen in everything from marble sculpture in ancient Greece through robotic surgery, right? Well, as soon as the AI-enabled design tool was implemented, junior engineers became optional in this process. Which means they mostly didn't participate. They were basically cut out of the action, for two reasons: first, novices are slower and make more mistakes, and second, experts have to attend to novices, which pulls those experts away from doing what they're best at. Removing novices from the work therefore improves speed and quality on two fronts.

But gains in efficiency and error reduction come with side effects. In this case, we are cutting workers who need to learn out of the loop in the name of increased expert productivity. In the short run, this is great—more and better chips, faster. And experts usually appreciate this shift, too—after all, they're getting to focus on "cooler" problems with less scut work. But even in the medium term, the organization and the profession build less skill because the expert-novice collaborative link is broken. Junior engineers don't get to be in the room—digitally or physically—to simply overhear and watch as senior engineers puzzle over a problem, and maybe even to pitch in with an extra set of eyes and hands. The result? A dramatic drop in healthy challenge, complexity, and connection, all in one fell swoop. And often it's even worse: those learners get redeployed to more isolating, basic work that offers more limited opportunities to develop their higher order skills. That junior engineer? To allow for a more efficient workflow, they get charged with running simulations for just one subcomponent of a chip. Then they become hyperspecialized, which means they never get access to the complexity and challenge associated with managing an entire chip's design. What's more, the very skills earlier generations of experts needed to learn as a matter of course may become obsolete, calling for a new measure of expertise and a new method for training novices to become experts. It's not just that the bond between novice and expert gets broken, but that the formula for expertise itself has to be partly reworked.

I've expanded my search to decidedly *un*intelligent technologies like videoconferencing, conveyor systems, and online labor platforms—everyday tools for everyday folks in a wide variety of organizations. Following the logic of the quote attributed to William Gibson, I expected the effects to be less intense and perhaps less painful, and that's exactly what I found. In fact, you have, too: just like Emily and her team, we've all lived it. Working virtually allows us to be more focused, eliminates or greatly reduces painful commutes, and dramatically expands our work-life flexibility. But we pay a subtle, profound price in skill and outcomes that flow from it, like lower morale, lower staff retention, less career development, and poorer task performance. Natalia Emanuel, a researcher with the Federal Reserve Bank of New York, and colleagues explicitly addressed this problem.[3] They studied an engineering firm and found that coders in the same building got 23 percent more feedback on their work than distant teammates—but that this shrank to 6 percent after their offices closed for the pandemic, resulting in a serious loss for novice coders trying to improve their skills.

At the same time, Emanuel and her colleagues found a boost in expert productivity similar to the one I found in my study of robotic surgeons: the less time one of their senior engineers spent with a junior engineer, the more productive the expert became. To double down on this, I'll share a troubling fact that I've never published: at one of the top teaching hospitals I studied, I analyzed six years of anonymized detailed medical records for robotic surgical patients. Statistical tests showed that for every medical resident in the operating room, patients spent 25 percent longer under anesthesia—a significant risk factor for serious complications like strokes. An average four-hour procedure involves two residents. So, if you take them away, that patient stays under anesthesia for 56 percent less time, or about two hours and fifteen minutes. Beyond increased risk to patients, leaving those residents in the room means an additional cost of $9,026 for the average hospital.

So, you can see why there's a compelling, short-term case for cutting novices out of the action when we implement new technologies. By virtue of the fact that they are still learning, we have to recognize that involving them increases risk and slows things down, and that there's an immediate upside in quality and profit if we let experts do their thing. But it also raises the question: How will the next generation of doctors, firefighters, programmers, teachers, lawyers, electricians, and filmmakers become experts themselves?

As the pandemic dragged on, research, old and new, underscored how important it is for us to physically gather at work. Showing up allows for the informal interactions that get us access to skills, and the results and opportunity that flow from it. And beyond fulfilling our need for relationality, in-person work has hard-edged benefits: for example, Jason Sandvik, a researcher then at Tulane University, and colleagues showed that when salespeople met in person for lunch to discuss sales strategies, it boosted their revenue by 24 percent for months afterward.[4] But the effects are collective, too—teams have more trust and make better decisions. Executives learn more about the front line, build empathy, and set better strategy. Part of the reason for all these benefits is the kind of vicarious learning we get working alongside those who know more than we do. So, while we were hard at work staying physically apart protecting each other from a pandemic, we were also inadvertently tearing down the hidden infrastructure for skill development.

Many companies took the "opportunity" that the pandemic represented to pause operations and look for new and better ways to invest in automation. To take one example: companies have invested much more aggressively in robotic process automation software—systems that learn how to do the menial "type, point, and click" work associated with entering and retrieving data out of corporate IT systems. This means little bits of job change for many people inside a large corporation. A few tasks gone here, a few modified there—once everyone adjusts a bit and irons out the kinks, there's a lot of time saved and improved quality in these processes. And the more these systems function, the more data they give to engineers who can then train these systems to better automate this kind of work. Which means more and more change for more and more people. None of this is necessarily bad. In fact, it might generally be fantastic—freeing us from dehumanizing administrivia. But whether it is good, bad, or somewhere in between, implementing systems like this always means job change, and job change always requires us to learn new ways to do things.

Job *change* is the trillion-dollar iceberg that could sink our *Titanic*.

Why? Change a job, you change ways of doing things. But those only deliver results if they're implemented reliably. And as long as there's a human doing the job, reliability only comes through skill. The kicker? We're betting the future of our species on the assumption that *billions* of us can build that skill through a taken-for-granted bond, just when we're hacking it apart. Let's take two comparable, recent research papers to flesh this out. In mid-2023, Rob Seamans, an economist at New York University, and colleagues published an analysis of the potential impact of AI like ChatGPT on all known jobs, as registered in a US-government-curated database on work called O*NET.[5] O*NET covers the work activities for 1,016 occupations, breaking these down into 19,265 tasks, like "immunize a patient" or "operate welding equipment." At the same time, Daniel Rock, an economist at UPenn's Wharton School, and colleagues from OpenAI published similar analysis.[6] Both papers aimed to show how much each and every job was "exposed" to the automation that a general-purpose technology like GPT-4 represents. Exposure here means how many of the fine-grained tasks in a job could get a 50 percent productivity boost if the worker used GPT-style technology.

These studies made the news right away. Many folks anchored on to the fact that a very few jobs were at or very near 100 percent exposed—like blockchain engineer and mathematician. We're drawn to black-and-white, "total" style change, for one. But also, it struck closer to home for the intelligentsia: it looked pretty clear that it was mostly white-collar workers who were most exposed to a new automating technology. But despite what some immediately claimed, this didn't mean those jobs were going away—it meant that someone in those jobs would have to *change* the way they did almost everything, if they used GPT-style technology. That would require almost complete reskilling. But those jobs are rare. The jaw-dropping scope of this reskilling problem becomes apparent when you read the conclusions in these papers that are perhaps less flashy. Try this one on for size: 80 percent of all working adults have jobs that are 10 percent exposed to GPT-style technology. In the US, that's 108 million people, and around the world, that's 2.7 *billion* people who might need to relearn 10 percent of their job.

If this finding doesn't give you pause, consider this: all that billions-scale exposure and potential change is just from the "mind" side of the human skills ledger. Those two studies only considered tasks that were subject to automation by software that deals with ideas, writing, images, and thought. Yet we're also making rapid progress on the "muscles" side of things through AI-enabled robotics. Have you seen Boston Dynamics' dancing, parkour-loving humanoid robots do their thing? If you haven't, put this book down and watch a recent video to get a reset on what's possible. And look to startups like Agility Robotics, Figure, and even Tesla for humanoid systems that are getting close to ready for real work in settings like warehouses. That's to say nothing of the many dozens of AI-enabled nonhumanoid robots that I've been studying around the US for the last four years: these aren't prototypes. They're being put to work at scale. Erik Brynjolfsson, a Stanford economist, Daniel Rock, and I are working on a rubric to estimate the exposure of physical tasks to these developing technologies. Preliminary results make it clear that many, many physical tasks in the O*NET database will be exposed to profit-generating robotic automation in the very near term. It might not be quite as much as with software alone—robots are expensive, compared to ChatGPT—but millions more people will be exposed, and in many cases, they'll be in more physical jobs that would not have been all that affected by GPT-style automation. So, it turns out that a 10 percent job change for 2.7 billion of us is probably a *significant* underestimate.

Historically, adjusting to a 10 percent job change is no big deal for an individual. It rarely requires getting a new degree, a new certification, or even taking a course. In fact, employers probably won't pay for it or even notice. We get a little formal training and then we figure it out. From each other. On the job. That's how it's worked for probably 160,000 years, and we could count on it to help all of us adapt. We took it for granted.

We can't anymore.

STANDING STILL IS NOT AN OPTION IF YOU'RE ON THE TRACKS

You should be able by now to hear two economy-scale trains rumbling down the tracks toward us, from opposite directions. From one side comes the "reorg" train: technologies that allow us to change bigger-scale things about how the work gets done, like who sits where, how roles and functions interact, and what we measure. Over the last thirty years we have fragmented our collocated workplaces to take advantage of tools like videoconferencing, cloud computing, and labor platforms, and we're awash in analytics on everything from security to employee health. In two years, the pandemic has fast-forwarded us through ten or fifteen more. From the other side comes the "technique" train: technologies that allow us to perform work differently—ChatGPT for writing, robots for moving boxes, and smartphones for sales. In our search for increased productivity, we are aggressively developing and deploying new tools—adding new engines to each train.

If you strip away the particulars, a single finding emerges: when either kind of technology allows an expert to become more effective and focused, we buy it and we use it. Organizations and experts simply do not pass up improved productivity. But in pursuit of almighty productivity, we are embracing these technologies in ways that reduce meaningful involvement for millions of workers throughout the global economy. The more we load up the reorg train, the more control we grant to individuals, managers, and leaders to carve up an organization and reassemble it. That crashes into the novice-expert bond. Meanwhile, the more we load up the "technique" train, the more experts are motivated to turn their focus inward and work alone. That crashes into the expert-novice bond, too. Over time, novices are becoming increasingly optional and distant participants in an experts' daily tasks. Experts are also missing out: on feedback from the front line, the subtle but critical task of paying it forward to the next generation, and the sense of fulfillment that mentorship brings. Healthy challenge, complexity, and connection are under threat from both directions.

For now, the threat to skill may not feel urgent for most of us, even if we can hear the distant whistle of these trains coming down the tracks. But the bind in most people's jobs—maybe yours—is that we tolerate incremental degradation of the three Cs. Work from home? Can do. Analyze on your own? Sounds faster. Do surgery with a robot by yourself? Great. The seductiveness of technologically enabled productivity should make all of us concerned about our adaptability as a species. One of the most valuable tools in our toolbox—the bond between expert and novice—is being compromised for short-term wins, just when we need it most. Before we know it, at least 2.7 billion of us will be running to stand still.

Most corporations have yet to hear the whistle of the oncoming train. They spent just over half a trillion dollars on learning and training in 2022, but almost none of that was spent on the expert-novice connection. This is clear from the fact that we don't even measure our efforts to foster novice learning alongside experts. And yet most organizations depend heavily on this informal, apprenticeship model. A 2011 Accenture survey revealed that only one in five workers felt they had learned any new job skills through formal training in the previous five years.[7] Paul Osterman, a researcher at MIT, recently did a far more rigorous survey, representative of the US working populace—only half those surveyed received *any* training, and that's including those who went out and found it themselves, without employer help.[8] We've just happened to set work up in ways where an expert relies on a more junior member of their occupation for help, and we take it for granted that the junior member learns in the process. You can find rare exceptions in a few occupations where failure is not an option: EMTs, cops, surgeons, electricians, and so on. They have well-developed apprenticeship and certification standards. But even there, they stop after an initial training period is over, even though experts would tell you that they built critical skill *after* they headed out on their own. If we spend half a trillion dollars on formal training a year—if that's what success in formal training is worth to us—how much should we be spending to understand and support the skill code that's the basis of the vast majority of our most valuable capabilities? One thing's for sure: it's not zero.

But here we are. Basically, giving no attention and devoting no resources to our adaptive lifeblood at the very moment we're thinning it out through the way we're handling technology. We can—and must—do better than this.

Fixing a problem takes seeing it clearly. That's why it's time to take a careful look at how this is playing out, through the lens of healthy challenge, complexity, and connection. This will give you a crystal-clear picture of this threat and the tools to help you know it when you see it in your work or organization. Let's start with challenge.

THE THREAT TO CHALLENGE

Meet Amber. She's a certified OR nurse with fifteen years' experience, earning six figures, and she's bored out of her skull: today's a robotic surgical day.

Pan around the OR and you'd see an intricate, temporary marvel: a three-part, 2,500-pound robotic surgical system, connected via coaxial and fiber-optic cables, covered in sterile drapes, reaching into the patient via four sticklike surgical instruments; a surgical "boom" extending down from the ceiling, repositioned to supply mission-critical resources like sterile water, carbon dioxide, and power; an anesthesiologist's "cart" at the patient's head, with an assistive breathing machine, a computer-controlled drip to manage the flow of anesthetic, and a display module to keep track of the patient's vital signs; a surgical scrub's station, next to the patient, constructed out of adjustable surgical instrument stands, each holding dozens of items from sutures to robotic instruments to tissue bags; and of course the patient table, set to give the robot space to function, mounted with procedure-specific padded braces and stainless steel struts that hold the patient in place. You'd see the surgeon at the console, operating away, the anesthesiologist intently monitoring vital signs, the scrub getting out a new surgical instrument . . .

And you'd see Amber, about ten feet away from all of this, sitting at a PC in the corner of the room, checking Facebook with her chin in her hand. Partly, she's just not engaged. She told me: "[working with the] robot is so boring, you sit there in the dark, and fall asleep." The surgeon operates very independently, and the scrub handles the few necessary tasks like swapping instruments. But partly, she's also tired and stressed. Everything you saw above? She and a surgical scrub had forty-five minutes to set it all up—connect and move equipment, reach up six and a half feet to cover the robot with sterile drapes, lay out instruments, turn on devices, the whole nine—but the work really takes an hour. That means she's racing the whole time and is usually sweating through her scrubs by the time it's done. The surgeon's not there to chat with and learn from and the work is repetitive, involving lots of checklists and data entry. And she's stressed because she knows she only has thirty minutes to break it down.

This is not what she signed up for.

It took Amber six years to work her way into the OR. She's always wanted to be an OR nurse. For one, the pay is great, but the main thing that got her there was surgery. In an open procedure, she set things up, sure, but there were fewer things to deal with, and most of them were "dumb" metal tools like scalpels, retractors, sutures, and so on. Certainly no computer-controlled surgical apparatus with fourteen different cable connections and four sterile drapes to set up every day. Pretty quickly after setup, the procedure got started, and she moved a lot between her desk and the operating table. She had to be ready—to get a surprise item, change settings on key equipment, and so on. But maybe even more important, she and she alone had to be ridiculously, almost aggressively proactive and deliberate about watching the work and maintaining a steady flow of instruments, materials, and waste to and from the surgical table. She had to be thinking four, five steps ahead, keeping tabs on how fast and well the surgery was going, so she could drop exactly the right items onto the surgical scrub's instrument table at the right time, in the right way so that they didn't even have a chance to think that they might need it. The items were just there. Waste products were just . . . gone from surgeons' and scrubs' view before they had a chance to think about asking for them to be gone. And away from the action, Amber was staging these things, getting them ready in phases so that when it was time for her to move them into or out of the surgical space, she only had to take the smallest action—pick it up and move it a foot or two. Beyond this, she had to manage all the information associated with the procedure—not a lot of work, but a steady trickle of data reading and entry about the patient, surgical progress, outcomes, and so on. Just one more plate to keep spinning, all while keeping a careful eye and ear on how the actual surgery was going.

She can't quite explain it, but working in a close-knit team that helps save people's lives by cutting them open . . . well, that's just a thrill. It takes a lot of skill and earns a lot of respect. Before the robot hit the scene, sure, she had a fair amount of setup work to do, but it was manageable. She still had meaningful time to connect with the patient and the family ahead of time, to gab and gossip with the scrub or the anesthesiologist as she worked at a steady but manageable pace. But she was generally in constant motion during the procedure, and that's what she liked. Her expertise was needed for everything from changing settings on equipment like a cautery device, to scrambling for an improvised mix of pads, sutures, and gauze when someone knicks an artery, to maintaining a smooth, relaxed flow of communication across the job functions in the room. She had to pay fierce attention, she had to be ready. Being an OR nurse was dirty, dangerous, and therefore challenging work, and she loved it.

Whether they believe robots are going to create or destroy jobs, most experts say that robots are particularly useful for handling "dirty, dangerous, and dull" work. They point to jobs like shutting down a leaky nuclear reactor, cleaning sewers, or inspecting electronic components to really drive the point home. Robots don't get offended, they are cheap to repair when they get "hurt," and they don't get bored. It's hard to disagree: What could possibly be wrong about automating jobs that are disgusting, mangle people, or make them act like robots?

Let's be clear: it's often great for the expert who uses the new technology directly. Intelligent technologies are usually designed to extend the expertise of someone involved in the work. If you're a civil engineer specializing in sewer integrity, you used to get key data from workers who crawled into a city's sewage system. They would take a half day to take a few photos and write up some comments, then would write up or dictate a report. Then you had to interpret all of that and make a judgment call on whether the current preventative maintenance plan was sufficient. Now? Those same workers lower a robot into the pipe, it crawls along, scans the tunnel walls with radar, infrared, and other sensors, captures video, and might even send that data to a program that analyzes this output to offer you interpretation, predictions, and suggestions. Thanks to these robots, you feel like you can trust this data more and can focus on more valuable, strategic analysis. You win. The city wins. The citizens win.

But it turns out—just as in Amber's case—that deploying intelligent technologies often deprives workers of the challenge they need to grow their expertise. I've now seen this across all my own studies—from warehousing to health care—and the dozens of other studies I've gone through with a fine-tooth comb. Use AI to analyze social behavior on the web, and doctoral students lose the chance to learn stats and coding. Use a robot for surgery, and surgical trainees end up watching, not learning. Use a robot to transport materials, and workers that handle those materials lose the chance to interact with and learn from the recipient. Use a robot to farm, and farmers end up barred from repairing their own tractors. Like Amber, they're bored out of their skulls—and their skills suffer.

If we do nothing, many millions of us will end up in the same boat.

THE THREAT TO COMPLEXITY

Arnold works on a kitting line in a warehouse, like the one you saw in Sita's facility: take one of each item, add it to a box going down a line, then close it up and ship it off to the customer. Last Thanksgiving, he had robotic blinders put on.

He and his coworkers clock in every day, then walk to the new robot line to take their positions—between robots, about ten feet apart from each other. These robots are basically arms with six joints and a grasper, mounted to a box that contains a computer that controls their actions. Arnold, his colleagues, and the robots face the fixed line—and the line is lagged into the concrete with steel bolts to ensure robots can get a precise fix on the conveyor, the products, and the bags they are supposed to go into. Once the entire getup is turned on for the day, bags come down the line, just like in Sita's warehouse, but Arnold and his coworkers' job is to tend to the robot, not do the pick-and-pack work. Partly that means feeding it: they watch the spring-loaded bin next to it to see when it is running low on product, then go to fetch more. But it also means covering for the robot when it makes mistakes. If it can't get an item into a bag in three tries, they make sure the item gets in there by hand. Or if the robot drops an item, they pick it up and finish the job. Or if it hits a bag or really gets stuck, they press the big, red emergency stop button on the robot and the line lead or an engineer comes over to restart things. It all moves pretty quickly, though, and there is pressure to keep the line moving, so he stays focused. Every slowdown counts against the day's numbers, and his incentive pay depends on those numbers staying high.

The way the line is set up, Arnold and his coworkers are physically separated from each other, and the robots themselves block the view from station to station. The noise that the whole system makes isn't medically dangerous but is definitely loud enough to drown out conversation. Practically, this means very little chitchat about the work. On top of that, Arnold's focus and the physical setup mean his eyes don't much wander toward his coworkers' stations and he can't often see others' mistakes. They just come his way, already kitted. He also doesn't get the benefit of watching the way others pack, stock their robots, or deal with product. And because he just walks to get one product and comes back with it, he doesn't get to watch or learn from a human who can tell him their thought process behind managing inventory across multiple lines. If this was a normal line, at some point he might have wanted to step into a "replen" role like that, a step up to a position where he would be responsible for keeping many kinds of bins full while tracking inventory. But the new arrangement means he can't see or help with the work the higher-skilled positions are doing. He just watches the robot take product out of its bin, stocking it back up and cleaning up after it when it makes small mistakes.

Arnold had become an isolated robot's assistant. In fact, he felt a bit like a robot himself.

The work was very different before advanced automation arrived. Arnold, his bosses, and his colleagues designed and ran the line.

The area leader would get new product, bring it in, and work with each line lead to come up with a plan for breaking down the components and kitting them together, and each line lead would bring that plan to their line. Then they'd work with folks on the line to figure out how to set up the tables, replenishment routes, and walkways to suit the product process. For the first few days, leaders and workers watched, adjusted, and improved until they reached a good system. Everyone got to see part of this process, and many got to participate. And they got to work, standing just a few feet from each other. Looking up and down the line to track products, mistakes, defects, and so on. Sometimes Arnold could see a problem three workstations away. This was also easier because he and his coworkers rotated across job positions and watched each other work. For instance, when he first started the job he'd learned how to be more efficient from his coworker Tuya. The way she held her hand directly above the line instead of moving it back and forth saved time and arm strain, a lesson Arnold was grateful for. The longer Arnold worked like this, the more he learned—not just about how to do his particular job, but about everything it took to run a line like this.

When the robots arrived, his organization worked very hard to simplify the kitting work so robots could put objects in bags at maximum speed with the fewest defects. Everyone involved was well intentioned and skilled. In Arnold's company and many others like it, managers, engineers, LEAN (aka "process improvement") experts, and even human resource professionals get expensive training to make work processes safer and more profitable. One key target in this work has different names, but their techniques all amount to one thing—reducing the number of times a human has to handle the product and limiting the amount of skill required for those tasks. In repetitive, manual industrial work—common in industries like warehousing, manufacturing, and electronics assembly—this is called "reducing skilled touches." Robots are great for these redesigned processes—they do the same thing, over and over, quickly, and with very few mistakes. And lower skill requirements mean that an untrained worker can get the job done at industrial reliability standards while the robots do their part. We know already that successful businesses can hire more workers because they do this work aggressively: those studies of robot adoption in chapter 1 make it clear that automators grow and add jobs. The trouble here is that complexity takes a beating for people in Arnold's job. The longer they stay, the more hyperfocused they have to be on a simpler and simpler task, and the less they get a sense of the broader work system they're embedded in. Good luck learning there.

These findings are not unique to Arnold, or his warehouse. They're playing out all around the US, in warehousing companies large and small. Remember, my team and I spent just over three years studying the implementation of AI-enabled robots in repetitive manual work at over a dozen warehouses around the United States. We had eight vendors onboard, all creating different robots and AI for slightly different applications. We harvested boots-on-the-ground data on each of these warehouses—before, during, and after these advanced robotic systems were implemented. We stayed in these warehouses all the way through the Covid-19 pandemic, right alongside the managers, workers, engineers, and vendor personnel who had to stick around to get us all the stuff we were no longer willing to go to the store for.

Our current technological upheaval is unique because of its velocity and diversity. Look at fulfillment operations. Just ten years ago, most companies were barely instituting building-wide systems to track inventory, and work was highly manual; five years ago we had workers walking computer-generated routes to pick product, and robots were moving goods to workers for them to pick; and now a central, AI-driven system is planning, tracking, and actually physically creating the flow of goods into and through the building through armies of diverse robots that can crawl up storage racks, grab an item, scurry down the floor, and hand them off to another robot for packaging. We need fewer and fewer humans to get the job done, and they're left in the crevices between these increasingly automated processes—in jobs that have been deskilled to their limits.

So, across all these sites, all this technology, all these companies, all these regions, we found that automation separated people from each other and kept them focused on discrete, mundane, and repetitive work—away from healthy complexity.

Yet as much as we may see these jobs as dehumanizing, low-paying, or deskilling, they are increasingly plentiful. They pay better than retail and other service jobs, and many of us depend on these jobs to provide for our families and make ends meet. In a very tangible way, we have automated a lot of people into these jobs, and many of them are at the end of their proverbial rope when it comes to work, skill, and career prospects.

The threat to complexity we've seen in warehousing shows up in all the latest field research on very different kinds of intelligent technologies, too: systems are installed to improve productivity, and the scope of human perception and action gets narrowed. I found surgeons spending their time in an immersive console focusing on a postage-stamp-sized piece of tissue—they couldn't see their staff, the patient's body, or anything else in the OR, so they can't directly assess and manage critical parts of the work anymore. They can actually lose skill as a result. Researcher Sarah Brayne found cops walking an algorithmically generated beat without understanding the rationale for it.[9] This can compromise their ability—even desire—to take in the complexity of a situation or neighborhood to do their own independent threat assessment. Another researcher, Ben Shestakofsky, found startup executives outsourcing customer service to the Philippines and losing direct contact with customers as a result.[10] Reading typed reports of customer complaints or—even worse—just statistics on customer preferences is no substitute for a real person with real needs, trying to give you feedback. All of us are losing access to the complexity that allows us to act skillfully, just as the world becomes increasingly complex.

If we want a world where working hard today offers a more skill-ful tomorrow, we need to do better.

THE THREAT TO CONNECTION

Casey is a medical resident, doing her six-month rotation through a postsurgical ICU—or what locals call "the SICU." At 5 p.m. all other doctors leave, she takes over the unit, and a feeling of dread washes over her: it's a robot night.

The SICU is an intense place, even without the robot. Patients were all, in the local lingo, "very sick"—often unconscious, venti-lated, and on a range of life-sustaining machines and drugs. They were highly unstable, too: their temperature, heart rate, and other vitals shifted regularly; they might spontaneously "crash" (enter cardiac arrest), gain or lose consciousness, excrete too much (or too little) fluid, struggle against their ventilator . . . the list was end-less. Without near-constant attention, patients could deteriorate and die. That's why each one had a separate sealable room and a dedicated, highly trained nurse. Everyone knew their main job was to stabilize these patients so that they could walk the long road to recovery. And Casey knew that this was all on her shoulders from 5:01 until doctors came back at 6 a.m. the following morning. The main thing she had to deal with right now, though, was getting ready for night rounds. At 9 p.m., the unit's attending physician ("attending" for short) would "beam in" to the body of a four-foot-tall mobile telepresence robot—with a screen and two cameras where its head should be—and drive with Casey from room to room. Think videoconferencing on wheels and you've got the pic-ture: the attending could turn the head to look around, could zoom in, and had two-way audio communication, so they discussed and examined each patient with their nurse and settled on patients' overnight care plans as they went.

Sounds helpful, right? Especially when you learn that the prior standard was a private landline phone chat between the resident and the attending. No checking on patients. No talking to nurses. No independent data for the attending: just take the resident's word for it.

Thing is, this was terrible for Casey's skill development. Right from the first robot night, Casey became irrelevant to most bedside conversations: the attending just spoke with the nurse. Casey spent from 7 to 9 p.m. poring over electronic health records and making notes, remembering how the day went and coming up with detailed overnight plans for each patient. Almost without fail, when they wheeled up to each patient room, the attending would start asking questions straight to the nurse that only they could answer and looking at the patient directly—to get very up-to-date information that Casey didn't have. She white-knuckled her notes, stuck to the protocol, and tried to keep the conversation focused—and didn't ask any of the questions she normally would in a private phone call. The nurses were looking for reasons to take her down a peg, and she wasn't about to look stupid. And the attending was too busy talking with the nurse about the patient's real-time status to ask the resident any questions or suggest alternative explanations. Often Casey ended up just standing there like a post, feeling foolish. So, overnight, she gave "compliance without understanding," in the words of one attending: she really didn't track the reasoning behind key clinical decisions and held to them rigidly. Nurses had to work around her to deal with emergent patient issues. By morning, the patients were fine—the direct nurse-attending consult saw to that—but Casey was drained and demoralized.

Before the robot, things were different.

At 9, Casey's attending would call, and counted on Casey to be ready with solid information. But Casey couldn't go get it on the spot—she was tethered to a central desk via the corded phone. Casey wanted to impress them and to earn their trust, so she walked bed to bed to gather information ahead of time. She talked with the nurses and looked at patients. She anticipated objections, contingencies, and questions, but more importantly she made small adjustments to patients' care and ordering labs. And she did this collaboratively with nurses, so they usually ended up on the same page. By the time her attending called at 9, Casey knew her patients cold and had nudged all of them toward even better health. She was whipped, but ready. So night rounds via phone were a radically different affair. She'd report out, bed by bed. For about one in five, she'd just say "bed [3], they're stable" and move on—no detail, no explanation. And 85 percent of the time (yes, I counted, every night, for the fourteen months I was there),[11] the attending took her word for it—on all the other patients, Casey was offering hypercredible detail and evidence of smart decisions made jointly with nurses. They reserved their conversation for puzzles and serious concerns. And since it was private, Casey felt safer asking "dumb" questions and her attending took more time to coach. By the end, she and her attending had more trust in her independent skill, and Casey had earned the respect that came with that. Trusting Casey's skill and respecting her effort is what allowed that attending to sleep at night or decide if they had to come in.

On the first robot day, she tried a lot of these tactics, but they all fell flat. Why do all that prep if the doc's just going to talk with the nurse anyway? By the end of the night, she learned how to play a new embarrassing game called robot rounds, one she was destined to lose.

For decades, we have been using intelligent technologies to get experts more focused on the core of the problems they are trying to solve. Using AI to analyze reports from cops on the beat lets patrol chiefs deploy their workforce in ways that cut crime and save lives. Getting data feeds from machinery allows repair engineers to predict maintenance needs. Automatically scraping and analyzing corporate financial reports allows senior bankers to present merger-and-acquisition deals far sooner and more credibly for their clients.

And telepresence robots allow remote doctors to directly diagnose patients and direct local care. These results are amazing and expanding fast. Why shouldn't we be thrilled about them?

Because, just as in Casey's situation, we're using intelligent technologies to connect experts to problems in ways that break the vital connection between novices and those experts. Give chiefs automatic crime predictions and beat cops lose their trusting relationship driven by joint discovery. Allow engineers to diagnose technical trouble remotely and local techs only get to help solve them once or twice a year instead of every week. Automate basic financial analysis and junior bankers become "script monkeys" who can never prove themselves in side-by-side work with their mentors.

Intelligent technologies are like gas on this fire. They are so flexible and cost-effective that by building them we've given ourselves new, easy-to-use, high-impact tools to redesign the work. For decades, reconnaissance pilots and their colleagues had to change the way they worked to accommodate new technology, but the changes were so coarse and slow that they had time to adapt. They could add new responsibilities and new skill sets—like bulky aircraft control and night flight—adjust their collaborative patterns—like sharing tasks across a larger crew complement and building new techniques for communicating across that crew—and seek new results—like extending flight time and flying above enemy radar. But all of that relational reconfiguration was possible because the pace and intensity of change was slow enough, even though it might have seemed fast up close.

But now an organizational investment in intelligent technology means exceptionally rapid reconfiguration of an entire system of human connection. This can literally be lightning-fast: automated high-frequency trading systems can both execute trades and learn from them faster and more efficiently than a human can even comprehend. The surgical robot means that, overnight, you've got to reshuffle the entire OR task structure, top to bottom. In some cases, the expert ends up in a boring job because the system is so well tuned to circumstance. Or, more commonly, the work required to support that expert becomes so routinized that direct collaboration isn't much needed anymore, so support workers end up hustling around the edges, away from the action and meaningful human connection with the experts involved. And if you're a novice occupying one of those support roles, hoping to build trust and earn respect, well . . . you're in trouble. Experts pay a slow, hidden price, too: a critical part of the meaning in work flows through paying it forward to the next generation, getting the satisfaction of seeing them succeed with less and less of your help, and crowing about them to others. All that fades away, and you're left more isolated and less fulfilled. In fact, everyone can feel that way. Remote work alone can drive this outcome, and all this may be a key reason why in May 2023 the US surgeon general issued a first-ever, eighty-one-page advisory on what they call an "epidemic of loneliness and isolation."[12] We spend most of our waking hours at work, and if human connection becomes unhealthy there, skill might not be all we lose.

None of this is necessary, but it is happening. There's very big money to be made by sacrificing connection on the altar of productivity, and the expert job is a lot easier with intelligent technologies in hand. And while I've dissected that one C at a time, you can see throughout this chapter and probably in your own work that these kinds of technology-driven changes affect all three Cs, all at once. The threat to skill is total. It might not have hit you yet, or hit in any serious way, but the economic and technical conditions are ripe for economy-scale automation in all kinds of jobs in the relative near term. GPT-style AI is inbound for more intellectual tasks, and robotics are on their way for the physical work. And we are rapidly making these technologies more capable, flexible, inexpensive, and responsive. In fact, we're building them so they can—increasingly—improve themselves with less and less help from us.

So here we are: healthy challenge, complexity, and connection are on the ropes, and it's all our own doing. And the more we do this, the more we sacrifice our "meta superpower": the ability to build new skills we need to handle the world we're so rapidly creating.

Scared, or depressed? I can't say I blame you. But before you get too worked up, remember, this is not a doom-and-gloom book. I bring more data and research that definitively shows you can have faith—in both us and our technologies . . . but only if we learn from it and put it to work. Next, I'll get us started on that journey by introducing you to some crafty, literally "deviant" people among us who have found new ways to build skill in spite of all these threats. That's right: our willingness to do inappropriate things turns out to be a saving grace when it comes to these technothreats to challenge, complexity, and connection. The core insight is this: most people wouldn't dream of bending and breaking rules to build skill, but a few have. I've specialized in finding them, studying them, and distilling their tactics into practical insight for the rest of us. Understanding these "shadow learners" very carefully gives us the beginnings of a new skill code vocabulary—the very first step toward reworking it for the twenty-first century. Let's turn to them now.

CHAPTER SIX

LEARNING FROM THE SHADOWS

emember Arnold on the kitting line? He and most of his coworkers were in the same boat: the longer they stayed on the robot line, the less skill they had. They were literally getting deskilled by working hard.

Except for Inés. After just a couple of weeks dealing with the system, she'd become a budding robotics expert and made a patentable suggestion to improve every robot on the line.

In many ways, she was just like the rest of her coworkers assigned to this futuristic kitting operation. For one, Inés spoke only Spanish. She had fled Honduras as a teen and settled in the Central Valley of California. Her lack of proficiency in English wasn't a big deal for this job; the work was highly physical, and visual demonstration was often enough to get everyone trained, oriented, and ready to get to work. Even she and her coworkers didn't all share a language. So, when they had trouble understanding, she and her coworkers relied on Eduardo, their multilingual line lead. Inés had the equivalent of an eighth-grade education and had held only simple jobs before this one—she and her family were fully occupied with their safety and plans to flee for about three years before she arrived in the States, and there was no time for school or training. And before the robot and after, she physically did her kitting job just like everyone else: deal with inbound product, make sure it gets into the bag moving by her station, keep an eye out for defects, and help with problems when they come up.

But in other ways, she was special. When everyone else was heads down, doing their jobs, she'd slow her work as her eyes wandered off the line to the robot sitting next to her. A no-no. During breaks, she'd leave late and come back early to watch the engineers resetting the bots and troubleshooting error codes. That raised some eyebrows from coworkers. And when the robots threw those error codes during live production, she'd study them and their small screens, even waiting a few extra seconds before calling Eduardo or hitting her red e-stop button. She definitely shouldn't have dawdled there. She never got in trouble for these things, and they never seemed to hurt production, but they were at best a little . . . odd.

Then one day, at break, Inés asked to talk with Eduardo. She had an idea.

She walked him over to the line and pointed to the tablet-style screen attached to its base. This was where the error codes showed up that were designed to help those nearby identify and resolve what the engineers called "exceptions"—problems with robotic tasks such as object recognition and grasp detection. Each kind of error code offered instructions for a specific kind of fix, and she and her coworkers had to respond and deal with it. And that's where the problem came in: the codes were displayed in English. Sure, some of her coworkers intuited the meaning of some of these codes, but only she knew them all. That wasn't because she knew how to read them—she was just paying fierce attention and deducing what the error codes meant. But there was deeper trouble because the codes changed as the system improved: new products came in and engineers reworked robots' routines for detecting, grasping, and "inserting" (that is, dropping) items. Inés was the only one who was able to keep up, and she was barely treading water. She offered Eduardo a fix: switch to picture-based prompts. Robot can't grab? Show a drawing of the robot with an X through its bin. Robot can't drop? Show one with the robot with the X through a product bag. The upside seemed clear: reduced training time, improved quality control, and better data labeling for the AI that underlay the robotic picking system.

Within a day, Eduardo shared—but did not credit her for—this suggestion with the vendor's engineering team. They implemented the change within a week, so workers were able to handle exceptions and robotic resets more rapidly and reliably. And she didn't object: it didn't even occur to her that she had done something noteworthy. Her job was to help the work go better, and in her mind that's what she did.

For a moment, set aside the fact that she didn't get recognition or pay for her patentable suggestion. Set aside the fact that she didn't think she was doing anything special. Yes, in a more just world, she would have. But this kind of contribution gets overlooked all the time. In fact, if I had just relied on interviews with those who could speak English, I'd have missed this, too. I just happened to be there to watch her make her suggestion to Eduardo.

She got something valuable out of the situation that no one could take from her, however: technical skill. To make her suggestion, she had to find a new way to learn, without help, and against the rules. She had to understand the basic kinematics—or movement capabilities—of these robots. She had to understand the relationship between those movements and the prompts that came up, so she had built some know-how about computational logic. And she understood the connections between various prompts and the need for human intervention. In short, she had become a local robotic user-interface expert, without anyone noticing, and without permission. Inés was a shadow learner.

CHEATING TO LEARN

Bucking rules has always been a precious source of insight and innovation, not just skill. Some organizations have even come to embrace this paradox: in 1982, Hewlett-Packard gave its first award for "Meritorious Defiance" to Chuck House, an engineer.[1] His customer wanted a bigger monitor. His boss told him not to spend the money to develop it. Chuck did it anyway and came up with the flat screen. The customer put in a huge order, and the rest is history.

In fact, history is full of stories like this. Look at any significant breakthrough and you'll eventually find someone who was willing to strain against convention to see a new way. They might not have broken any laws, they might not have known what they were doing, but they definitely stepped outside the bounds of propriety to do something that no one had done before. This comes as no surprise to social science. In chapter 1 I introduced you to sociologist Robert Merton. A little over eighty years ago he published an article titled "Social Structure and Anomie," which proposed the idea that some of us turn to deviance to achieve goals when legitimate means fail.[2] A mountain of research has followed, verifying this view. If you want a little extra summer reading in this vein, pick up *Wayward Puritans* by Kai T. Erikson—a book-length study of rule breaking among some of the most pious people in history.[3] What counted as deviance for them would count as near-sainthood for the rest of us.

What's less well understood is that to achieve these innovative outcomes—big and small—the people involved had to build skill, too. There's a lot of "doing" behind any improvement, any breakthrough. Trying things out, failing, learning to do better, devising new techniques, applying them, teaching others—the list goes on. And just like the ultimate innovation outcome, building those skills—which we now know takes time and a lot of support—had to unfold in the shadows. Norms had to be violated. Rules broken. And sometimes, risks taken, and people hurt. This is shadow learning:

a messy hack for skill, born of necessity. Experts and novices both engage in it.

To see how it works, let's head back 150 years to Joseph Lister, the "father" of modern surgery.[4]

Before Lister, surgery was butchery.

Surgeons began to see infection as a serious problem in the second half of the 1800s. Ether and other general anesthetics had recently been discovered, and these eliminated the extreme pain from surgery. This allowed surgeons to work more meticulously and greatly reduced psychological trauma for all involved, but these technologies did not reduce patient mortality. What had always been true remained true: surgical fatalities were mostly due to complications of postoperative infection, such as gangrene, sepsis, and fever. Eliminating pain did nothing to change this. In fact, some now argue that general anesthesia extended operative time, exposing patients to more infectious agents—which increased postoperative infection. To add insult to injury (literally), compound fractures—the kind where the bone breaks the skin—skyrocketed in Europe due to the Franco-Prussian War and industrialization. All this drove overcrowding in continental hospitals, exacerbating the infection problem. One set of statistics (rarely generated in those days) makes the point. In 1872—right at the beginning of Lister's career—37–41 percent of compound fracture victims across all German hospitals later died from infection.[5] At the country's best hospital, in Munich, 80 percent of all wounds were infected by hospital gangrene. "Horrible was our trade!" a surgeon of the period declared. Everyone was desperate for a solution.[6]

The surgical profession couldn't deal with infections because it couldn't agree on what caused them. Some said that a chemical process caused infection, others a biological process, while others focused on "miasma," or noxious vapors from human waste and decaying flesh.[7] Nobody had or agreed on standards for data to support their claims, so these conversations went in circles. And critically, even where there was local agreement on a theory and the facts of postoperative infection, the tactics to address root causes were spotty and unskillfully implemented: some wards would open windows to the outside for increased ventilation, others would fastidiously clean the walls, floors, and sheets, yet others gave patients injections of nucleic acid to stimulate the immune system, and others began using caustic chemicals on wounds. Given the systemic and pervasive nature of the problem, a solution required a good theory but also skillfully performed techniques.

Then along came a dour-faced Quaker with fuzzy white sideburns who changed everything. Joseph Lister was a surgeon who had worked for years developing advanced skills in biochemistry and microscopy. One day he read about carbolic acid being used by farmers to treat their fields and that it had dramatically reduced death and disease in their cattle population. Betting that a diluted solution of the disinfectant could be used to treat wounds, he not only began to apply it to wounds, but he also used it to clean surgical instruments, even spraying the surgical theater with a fine mist. He conducted his first operation using carbolic acid in 1865, washing and draping all wounds with cloths soaked in it. Though his patient's wounds took four months to heal and involved frequent reapplication of acidified dressings, there was no infection. As he used it more, he treated the acid itself as a bit of an afterthought. In his writings, what mattered more was skillful technique, such as applying the acid to a wound every single time a dressing was changed without first touching a potentially contaminated object or person.

Just like that, he had invented antisepsis—a technique involving carbolic acid that stopped surgical patients from getting life-threatening infections. The mortality rate in Lister's Glasgow Royal Hospital was 46 percent in 1866. With his new methods, by 1877, it was 5 percent.[8] His work has saved millions of lives and Lister is now celebrated as the father of modern surgery.

Arriving at the world-changing breakthrough of antisepsis—refining and scaling Lister's antiseptic technique to hospitals around the Western world—didn't happen through a neat and orderly process of medically approved trial and error. They couldn't follow the usual routes to challenge, complexity, and connection. That would have required waiting for widespread approval, an experienced mentor, or an understanding of the important problems involved, for example. None of this was available. *No one* knew what they were doing, and it all looked dangerous. So, Lister and many other doctors broke with convention to practice the skills involved. They did unusual, outside-the-lines, and provocative things—in a gray area between safe and unsafe, appropriate and inappropriate, ethical and unethical. Occasionally their behavior even went dark: they broke their oaths and hid data, as people died or lost body parts.

For example, in Lister's own notes we learn of "Patrick F," a patient with a compound leg fracture—likely from factory work, the most common cause for such grievous injuries in those days.[9] Lister wrote that he applied a carbolic acid solution to the man's wound, but Patrick contracted gangrene anyway. Lister realized that the caustic effects of his own antiseptic measure were in fact a major—if not the sole—cause. That's right. Put too much burning acid on someone's skin and—surprise, surprise—it burns them, and that can get infected. From all appearances, Lister didn't secure Patrick's consent for this procedure, and at the time Lister did not have knowledge of proper technique, dosage, tools, and methods for assessing progress. He just tried it out. In the end, Patrick's leg had to be amputated. But Lister built skill. This is about as dark as shadow learning gets.

Despite many failures on Lister's part, groups of doctors picked up this technique based on imperfect information and tried it out on their own patients. They had the right idea—that acid could kill germs. But that's like saying salt is good on food. Except in this case, we're talking acid and a live human being. Surgeons overdid it, and the burns from this acid and the smothering dressings often accelerated gangrene, the very condition the technique was meant to treat. And yet these surgeons gained insight and built new skill. Lister had many such failures himself, but we wouldn't know his name if those early disasters hadn't paled in comparison to the successes. Obviously his methods weren't without ethical short-comings, but ultimately Lister and other surgeons mostly saved lives, perfected their technique, and shared their new knowledge. And eventually they rewrote history.

While we already know that revolutionary innovation such as antisepsis depends on webs of technique developed over de-cades, there is another, often-overlooked part of the process: the transgressive, even shadowy circumstances in which necessary skills and breakthroughs take root. It's a similar story with the Curies and the discovery of radium.[10] Tesla and the invention of the alternating current induction motor.[11] Adrià and the creation of molecular gastronomy.[12] Jobs and designing the iPhone. Yes, there's an invention at the end of the transgressive tunnel, but to get there, these experts and their collaborators had to build sig-nificant new skill in the dark, too.

Most of us won't do any "capital *I*" invention in our lives. But mil-lions of us are facing an exponential technostorm that is increasing barriers to approved, "normal" ways of building skill—as in the expert-novice bond. More broadly, new ways of working threaten healthy challenge, complexity, and connection. Yet the needs driv-ing our self-authored journey toward competence now run as deep as it gets. So, in one key way we're just like Lister: over eighty years of social science very clearly shows that some of us will break or bend the rules out of view to get the instruction, experience, and expertise we need to adapt, excel, and sometimes even change the world. In the language of this book, shadow learners have intui-tively worked out the skill code and found a way to rework it so they can keep building skill in spite of new barriers. That's great news: like the first to cut across a lawn between new buildings, they've been leaving tracks the rest of us can follow. For over ten years, I have focused my research on this shadow learning activity, both from the novice and expert point of view. We need their lessons more than ever.

SHADOW LEARNING FOR NOVICES

About a year and a half into my two-and-a-half-year study of robotic surgery, I brought key findings to my dissertation committee. I had found, across five top-of-the-line teaching hospitals, that most residents were struggling mightily to learn how to use robots, even though most of them had selected their hospitals because they wanted access to this technique that patients were clamoring for. It was the wave of the future . . . and they were stuck in the mud. I had overwhelming evidence for this skills morass and knew that it was because residents didn't get to operate anymore: the robot let the attending do the work without much help at all. I thought I had a slam dunk on my hands—my dissertation was done, right?

Not so fast, my committee told me. In fact, they said if I didn't do a whole lot more, I might not have anything worth publishing. They rightly pointed out that we had many studies showing things are hard with new technology. We "waste" enormous amounts of time, money, and well-being finding the right way to work new tools into preexisting kinds of work. So, while it was shocking to see in a context like surgery, it was predictable that residents would struggle to learn. With the wind spilling out of my sails, I mentioned that across my five hospitals I had found three residents who seemed to be doing great on the skills front—learning quickly and well, getting more and more access to the work, and so on. It also looked like they were doing it in similar ways. Beth (remember her, in chapter 1?) was one of them. My committee said that was interesting. Not expected. Could I find more of them? Then I'd have something.

This was my new mission: with about a year left, I spun up an additional study across thirteen more top-tier hospitals around the

US, getting access to residents and attendings at each. The more I watched procedures, the more I hung out with residents, the more I interviewed everyone, the more it became clear: about one in eight residents were successfully building skill relying on the same "deviant" practices as the three successful residents I had found in my original set of hospitals. And they weren't communicating with each other about their tactics: most thought they were doing unremarkable things to build skill and were on some level aware that their mentors and peers would probably judge their tactics as inappropriate. So, they kept it all to themselves. This was extraordinary: I had found residents independently adopting the same practices to build skill, but they were quite different from each other, and these hospitals had different attendings, different cultures, different training practices and standards. I've since found these practices in studies done by other researchers and in my own studies in other contexts, ranging from policing to data analytics. There are three of them, and each one represents a way that novices preserved healthy challenge, complexity, and connection in an environment that was incredibly inhospitable to skill development.[13]

The first of these I called *premature specialization*. What did this mean? Residents like Beth all specialized well before they "should" have, at the expense of their generalist education. In fact, they all started during medical school, before they had become residents. They might have skimmed organic chemistry to go to the robotics lab. Or "sacrificed" a normal hospital rotation to take on a research project with a robotic surgeon. One way or another, they found their way into experiences with robotically specialized experts. And no matter the specifics, these experiences were far too specialized from the point of view of the doctors and administrators who ran the institution: the point of medical school was to get training that would prepare them for any kind of practice. Ironically, when I asked, it was obvious to everyone that this made a huge difference for residents as they hit the ground in their residencies, so nobody seemed to judge them harshly. These residents' impressive readiness for complex work more than made up for their transgressions in previous years. For example, when he talked about a second-year resident who helped set up a research lab for robotic surgery during medical school, one attending told me: "I can already tell, she's great, she's better than most chiefs [sixth-year residents], but she spent significant amount of her life, like one to two years, in the robot lab at [hospital X] doing research, so it's like cheating, you know?" It's hard to argue with excellence.

I called the second shadow learning practice *digital rehearsal*. You can see the whole story in two quotes: "Watching a movie doesn't make you an actor, you know what I'm saying?" and "I watched that, I don't know, two hundred times for an hourlong video." The first one is from a chief of urology for one of the top teaching hospitals in the US. The second one was a resident at the same program. The chief spoke for tradition: everyone "knew" that operating was the way you were supposed to learn to operate. It was enshrined in "see one, do one, teach one." Research papers showed the critical role of "dwell time"—minutes in the OR—for surgical competence.[14] It was only right and proper to get your hands on a scalpel and in a patient to build skill. That was where a senior surgeon could mentor you, that's where you dealt with difficult choices, where to learn not to rush, how to lead the surgical team . . . the list goes on. In the culture of surgery, there's nothing better than learning in the OR. Which is why simulation and video were looked at as inappropriately "thin" ways of building skill. Anyone who relied heavily on them was focused on the wrong place, and was probably a fraidy-cat, a nerd, or both. They needed to peel their eyes away from the screen, pull on some scrubs, and get some blood on their hands.

The resident, on the other hand, spoke for progress and skill. He and the other shadow learners out there spent huge amounts of time carefully dissecting videos on YouTube as a way of complementing their learning in the OR. At first, they'd watch videos for familiarization: What am I looking at? What are the phases of this procedure? Then they'd move to assessing quality: How is this one going? Is it rough? Too pristine? Why? What techniques are being used, why, and are they working? They often made notes of all this, in some cases learning new software to annotate the video itself. And finally, they relied on their accumulated library of videos to "bone up" before a procedure. Were they going to do the anastomosis today (the intricate, difficult part of a prostatectomy where you suture the urethra back to the bladder)? They'd rewatch their favorite example at half speed, ten minutes before going in the OR. Sometimes, instead of YouTube, they used the robotic simulator in the hospital's training lab. The simulator was simplistic and abstract: you'd grab a digital hoop and try to move it along a virtual rope without touching it. More like a video game than real life by a long stretch. Still, they'd compete for high scores—sometimes only with themselves. It's important to remember that time on these activities—many hundreds of hours—was not only viewed as inappropriate and ineffective by some local senior experts, but it also took these residents away from other core responsibilities and relationships. Skipping lectures, or even night rounds on patients. Less time with their cohort, or even their formal mentor. A bit of a career risk when those experts were deciding who to favor for subsequent jobs.

And third, shadow learners found ways to create what I call *undersupervised struggle*. Remember reading the term "helicopter teaching" in chapter 2? The enemy of challenge? That was the soul-crushing everyday reality of mentorship via robot unless you did something to change the game. Many of them made the analogy to driver's education: the surgeon gave the resident the steering wheel but could hit the brakes at any time with a simple tap on a touchscreen. That, coupled with the fact that everyone in the OR could see the resident work at 10x magnification, meant surgeons gave a lot of verbal "help" and stopped the action repeatedly. It didn't take much to end up like Kristen did: control taken away, very loudly and publicly, after a steady stream of interruptions, corrections, and rhetorical questions.

To avoid all this and build skill, some residents found ways to operate with far less supervision. Some rotated to other, lower-status hospitals where senior surgeons weren't all that experienced with the robot. Or to departments within their own hospital that were newer to the robot. In either case, these attendings let residents like Beth operate a lot longer because they didn't operate with the robot all that often and couldn't tell what "great" looked like. They assumed these residents were well trained, and if they looked like they knew what they were doing . . . well, they even left the OR sometimes, allowing the resident to operate alone. Alternatively, some residents ended up working for "superstar" surgeons who ran multiple procedures simultaneously. How? By doing only the most difficult portions of a procedure and relying on residents to handle the rest . . . alone. Yes, as in the attending was not in the room. Seeing a pattern here? Two things were central: One, the resident was working near the edge of their capability. Extremely focused. Sweating in the console, even. But two, an attending was always available, so residents could pull on them for help. One resident who worked for a superstar said: "We were very good about not going rogue. Whenever you got stuck, the boss would come in and show you how to get out of it, or you'd call an upper-level resident, and they'd show you how to get out of it." Just on the off chance that your jaw isn't on the floor about all this, residents are definitely not supposed to operate without the attending in the OR. There's no law against this, but the American College of Surgeons strongly discourages it in general and forbids it in certain forms.[15] On top of all this, residents were risking reprimand—and placing patients at risk—just to learn the skills for their job. So . . . yeah, not exactly doctor-recommended material.

All three of these shadow learning tactics fostered healthy challenge, complexity, and connection, leaving new-on-paper residents with startling capability. Premature specialization provided early exposure to robotic surgery and involved increasing but managed exposure to the full scope of the tasks involved in the work. Complexity: check. But it also involved challenge: any practical exposure to surgical technique, even as a supporting player in a research lab, pushed a lowly medical student right near the edge of their capability. And it provided connection: you didn't get to "cheat" in this way unless a senior attending invited you in, and you helped them in ways that built trust, respect, and care. Digital rehearsal should ring all kinds of bells when it comes to healthy complexity. A resident who digested digital resources so deeply knew the robot and these procedures cold—they had seen them done ten different ways a hundred times. When they walked in the operating room, they were capable enough to digest far more complexity in the real work and make basic moves in more fluid ways. Interestingly, all their screen time allowed for healthy connection later: their level of "preloaded" fluency meant the novice could really bond with the expert on the job—by asking "smart" questions or even making suggestions, for example. And this fueled challenge. When this happened, the expert surgeon gave the novice stretch work almost right away and thought more highly of them and their capability. Even when the best experts had a hard time with sharing control if they didn't have to, shadow learners also pushed for more challenge. Remember, they were sweating it, but also had a new deal with experts: let me struggle and ask for help unless you see a red line getting crossed. This new deal helped them hit their optimal challenge points and got experts to provide scaffolding that was tuned to the complexity of the task. And so on: just picture the items on the healthy challenge list getting ticked off, one by one.

Against the rules and out of the limelight, these novices got the healthy challenge, complexity, and connection they needed to build skill. And it showed—they raced ahead of their peers and got the lion's share of the skill-enhancing work as a result. This was very

much a riches-to-the-rich scenario: if you walked in with significant skill compared to other novices, you got more access, you built
more skill, you got more access . . . and your peers sat watching
on the sidelines. But also, up close, all these tactics strained the
bounds of propriety: there's no way they'd be approved as a whole-
sale replacement of current best practice. Perhaps because of that,
challenge, complexity, and connection weren't ideal, either. These
shadow learning residents discovered and used their tactics in isolation. How much more trust, respect, and care could they have
built if they could be open about what they were doing with each
other and the experts around them? How much better could experts have directed residents' attention regarding the next layer of
complexity they could handle? And how much better could those
experts have done at scaffolding residents to their next level of surgical challenge? The answer's at least "some," here. None of this
was ideal.

My team and I saw shadow learning over the three and a half years
that we observed everyday work of entry-level folks in warehousing,
but it showed up in very different ways. Think back on Inés. Most
workers put their heads down and did their jobs. She was one of the
rare few—sprinkled throughout their organizations—who found
"deviant" ways to build skill in jobs that were aggressively deskilled
by their organizations.

At a high level, they all did this the same way: normal work routines presented similar problems on a regular basis. Nothing cata-
strophic, just bumps in the road. They just got irritated or curious
about them and tried out various fixes—without permission. In
fact, a good number of these fixes ran against standard operating
procedure. And because these problems occurred repeatedly, workers had a chance to refine their techniques. In other words, to build
skill. You already know about Inés, the budding user interface de-
signer. That's how this worked: people didn't just solve whatever
problem was in front of them. They demonstrated what we called
a "work sensitivity"—kind of like a Star Wars jedi who is sensitive

to the force, workers with a sensitivity would fixate on problems in a particular part of the work far more than most. Inés had a technology sensitivity, for example.

Gerardo had a mechanical one. He was one of a few dozen workers in a medium-sized warehouse that created, packaged, and shipped specialty Chinese foods like congee and rice from specific Chinese provinces. Even though he had the same formal responsibilities, title, and pay as all his coworkers, he had become the "fix-it" guy for the building. If the rice spinners or steamers broke down, if a conveyor stopped, if anything mechanical started to struggle, Gerardo got a yell, even though he wasn't supposed to leave his post. And even when he had never quite dealt with that specific problem before, he could usually get the offending machinery back on its feet. Gerardo didn't read manuals, had never taken a course, and didn't particularly think of himself as gifted in this way. But it didn't take long to find out how he got there and kept sharp: whenever experts came in to install, move, repair, or upgrade machinery, he was glued to them, asking questions, watching, and listening. And as he and his coworkers integrated that machinery into their daily flow, he watched it, listened to it, laid his hands on it as it ran—to get a feel for what "good" and "not so good" felt like. So, those experts almost never get a call for the same problem twice—Gerardo's got it covered.

This included the fancy new robots. Two of them were installed to arrange congee pails coming off the line and to send these into a shrink-wrapping machine. The worker at the shrink-wrapping station was told to supervise the first robot and the worker at the palletizing station was reassigned to mixing more porridge to take advantage of the increased production capacity that the robots offered. Gerardo troubleshot where the robots physically interacted with conveyors and the shrink-wrapping machine. Vendor engineers had built fixtures, grippers, and rails to handle congee buckets, and these solutions didn't function perfectly. Buckets sometimes arrived at the first robot slightly off-kilter because of sticky material on the conveyor belt, for example, and the robot couldn't handle these odd exceptions. And pads of packaged congee sometimes required a slight push after the robot put them in the opening to the shrink-wrapping machine, because its initial "grab" on them was imperfect. Gerardo's mechanical sensitivity led him to identify these issues and address them through minor physical changes like shimming the entry slide for the shrink-wrapper. Before he got to work on these problems, throughput and quality suffered, mostly because the worker at the palletizing station couldn't move to the congee filling area; they were too occupied handling these issues. Gerardo's solutions enabled the system to function as everyone had hoped, freeing up the palletizing worker to expand production.

Beyond technical and mechanical, we found workers developing skills related to people (say, dealing with conflict or informal training), work processes (figuring out how to get something done in fewer steps), and product quality (watching for damage or defects). But they were all doing it in the same way: get focused on a recurrent problem, try a solution in ways that color outside the lines of procedure, then refine it. The loss for everyone was that they were mostly in Inés's shoes: they didn't get noticed or get credit for their skill, so they couldn't parlay it into a better job with better pay. But the skill and initiative were there. A senior ops manager at one firm shook his head as he summed this up: "Talent flows through this building like water." If shadow learners were lucky, a good manager saw and encouraged their off-script experimentation. So, while they were rare, if they got noticed, these folks further developed their skills. Some even got promoted on that basis—in fact we found that this was the story for a small percentage of the executives at these companies.

Take a moment to appreciate the conviction and intuition that all this shadow learning requires. These folks were novices. They only got ahead by earning the trust and respect of those above them. And that took a long string of good behavior—remember from the chapter on connection how tricky good "comportment" is? So those few who found new, rule-breaking ways to learn were essentially risking it all—repeatedly—on a hunch. Did they know these tactics would work? No. Did they even have a theory that would help them understand whether they made sense? No. Was there real risk that they'd get "in trouble" if they were found out, or that they wouldn't get noticed—in some way limiting their career prospects? Absolutely. All of this represents a ridiculous high-wire act for your garden-variety novice. One in eight residents did okay. Inés and Gerardo didn't.

SHADOW LEARNING FOR EXPERTS

Meet Darren, a director at an investment bank. Though he's an executive, he's gunning for a managing director role—basically one of a small group of senior bankers at the top. His firm provides advice on capital markets to companies on major corporate transactions, such as mergers and acquisitions, as well as changes to capital structure like public equity and debt offerings. In small teams that include junior analysts and associates and senior members like him, Darren's firm does financial analysis to create pitch books that he then presents to clients. Aside from the shift away from pencil and paper to spreadsheets, the skills and techniques required for the work haven't changed much since Darren joined about twenty years ago. That is, until FactSet and CapIQ arrived. These tools gather data directly from online public filings, automatically calculate key metrics, and then feed these calculations directly into spreadsheets—what once took two hours now takes perhaps ten seconds. Large chunks of the work were now automatable, and everyone had to adapt . . . including Darren.

Darren saw this coming, saw an opportunity to distinguish himself, but was in a jam. He knew he would need to learn how to deal with these new tools, but he didn't have much time. He was focused on making deals and handling complex problems—his firm made money and built status when he put his skills to work. On top of that, part of his expertise was tied up with his personal status. More junior bankers looked up to him, trusted him because he was capable and confident. Looking like he was a learner all over again—messing up, asking silly questions, struggling on task— these were risky maneuvers for someone with a long way to fall in the eyes of others. So, he had to find another way.

He found it with Allen and Gaye, two junior bankers from other groups. Darren had reached out to a few other senior bankers, asking them to select one or more juniors to join Darren to build skill with these new tools. Allen and Gaye were "voluntold" to make the leap, though they were eager and had shown strong technical capability. And—unlike him—they were supposed to be learning new things and had nowhere to go but up in terms of status. Darren then arranged for the three of them to jointly figure out how to use FactSet and CapIQ in real client work. He directed the process, developing lists of metrics and quality standards that Allen and Gaye used as they developed spreadsheets and templates that others might use. They met regularly—daily, at first—to review the output and the process, and to imagine how the tools might be used and misused by others when they were more broadly available. Darren didn't spend a ton of clock time in these interactions—perhaps an hour a day, on average—but as he assigned them work, asked them naïve questions, looked at their inputs and outputs, and troubleshot problems side by side with them, he built strong skills with both systems. He looked and sounded like a fool sometimes, especially since on any given day they could handle the systems better than he could. But he had orchestrated their team environment to limit outside scrutiny, and they respected him for pushing to "raise the bar" on quality. By the end, he could run reports just about as well as they could, and knew more than they did about how to organize a team to take full advantage of these new tools. Now he was a stone-cold killer with the technology compared to his peers—their skills were firmly rooted in a world dominated by Excel and manual internet searches.

Darren succeeded in building skill through what Callen Anthony (at NYU) and I call an *inverted apprenticeship*.[16] This form of shadow learning involves reassigning novices in ways that allow an expert to build skill while saving face. As a form of shadow learning, however, inverted apprenticeships teach us a deeper lesson: your formal title and status don't always correlate with your expertise. Once you see this, you can see expert-novice relationships springing up in multiple directions, all over the place. Senior managers everywhere rely on their new, young hires to build skill with social media. Supply chain managers depend on young engineering grads to get savvy with satellite data. From the surgical theater to the warehouse, experts with new technology will be sitting in plain sight, but you might need to look past their titles to find them.

When experts run up against new technologies that they don't know how to use, they take one of four pathways: seeking, stalling, leveraging, or confronting. All of these are forms of inverted apprenticeship. But the results—for both expert and novice—are very different along each path.

Darren took a pathway we called "seeking," where the senior expert preemptively pulls promising novices away from their work, and all parties learn a lot by struggling together with the new technology. I saw this in robotic surgery, too, where residents were slack-jawed at the opportunity associated with this joint struggle with a senior expert. When I was interviewing a world-class robotic surgeon about his early robotic training, he smiled and said, "It was a weird time where my mentors who I really respected—we were working it out together, and all of a sudden, my input kind of mattered as much as theirs for this new work. How rare is that?"

Pretty rare, it turns out. Unfortunately, less than 10 percent of the experts in our independently collected datasets constructed an inverted apprenticeship that benefited both the expert and the novice. The rest of them created inverted apprenticeships in ways that boosted the expert's skills at the expense of the novice's learning and job quality.

For example, in the "stalling" pathway, surgeons who were perfectly satisfied with their current tools realized they couldn't rest on their laurels for the twenty or thirty years left in their career: the robotic wave of the future had arrived, and they had to adapt somehow. Their primary gambit was delaying, simplifying, and hiding their skill development. They found ways to build skill away from their normal work environment, for example, obscuring their departures from their home institutions and on-site training sessions with terms like *practicum* or *sabbatical*. They were learning, just away from their local colleagues. None of that was quite appropriate, and it all but eliminated any hope that residents might have to build skill with the new technology by collaborating with that mentor: they weren't home and didn't want to be found.

On the other hand, some senior investment bankers took a "leveraging" pathway, where they avoided using the technology, and treated it as a problem for novices to solve. They relied on junior bankers to surreptitiously teach them about the tools. Junior bankers didn't want to make the senior bankers look bad by revealing their lack of technical sophistication, so they taught them about the limitations of these tools by asking questions that made it look like they were the ones struggling to execute on senior bankers' very reasonable and intelligent (yes, that's sarcasm) requests. For instance, Andy, a senior banker, asked for a new kind of market analysis that the new software couldn't handle—it didn't have access to all the necessary data. To teach him about the technology while "telling him no without seeming to tell him no," Maeve and Adam, two junior bankers, asked for Andy's advice on "where else to look" for other tools that could do what he was asking. He couldn't, of course—there was no such technology. But status-wise this kept him in the expert seat. This taught him what the new tech *could* do. Bankers slowly built understanding of new tools this way, and started to issue more and more sensible requests, given the profound new power these tools made available to them and their firm. This doesn't look pretty, because it isn't. But it's still an inverted apprenticeship. The expert uses their power to rearrange their working relationships with novices in a way that preserves their status and helps them build at least some new skill. It's just that in leveraging, they built only a modicum of skill, but it required novices to scurry around like rats and bend over backward, too. They got better at sucking up but missed out on a whole lot of core banking skill.

The last inverted apprenticeship pathway was even rarer than the first. But as much as seeking was positive and constructive, this one—which we called "confronting"—was negative and destructive. For example, some surgeons wanted no part of robotics. They saw it as offering no improvement on their time-worn methods and tools, and they proactively and publicly disengaged from it, dragging residents along with them. They did this to mooch a little robotics skill: When they operated with residents, these attendings would aggressively quiz these novices on the details, merits, and drawbacks of the new technology. They'd make fun of them if they couldn't quite do "good old-fashioned" surgery, saying perhaps they needed the "training wheels" that the robot provided. I was in the operating room with one of these surgeons after he had learned that the robot canceled out hand tremors. He was watching a resident and said: "Boy, that's a terrible tremor you've got there, Doug. No wonder you like the robot." Every time a resident rotated through to work with them, they went fishing for just enough skill to better critique the tool among their peers and in public, and to knock a little "sense" into these residents for being so enamored with the new tool. So, confronting helped the expert build enough skill to critique the new method, but they put the novice in the hot seat to get it: unless they quickly renounced robotics, this seriously compromised novices' skill development and confidence in *both* old and new methods.

No matter how effective they are at building skill, inverted apprenticeships are an important discovery: they allow experts to protect their status and build skill, when their position and workload prevent them from learning in approved ways. But out in the wild, we should be wary of them: only one in ten experts managed to set up an inverted apprenticeship that left both them and novices better off when it came to skill. Most are not done mindfully, and they'll leave novices harried or cut out of the action, and the expert won't really build all that much skill. At the same time, the "seeking" pathway is a bright ray of sunshine. That's proof that, without guidance, a theory, training, or a mandate, some shadow learners out there will create inverted apprenticeships that uplift both the expert and the novice in one of the hardest situations imaginable: a radically new technology washing up on their shores. And the sunshine doesn't end there—it can't: that's just the one "positive" inverted apprenticeship that Callen and I could turn up in our data. There will definitely be more ways for a rising tide to lift all boats when it comes to inverted apprenticeships. We just need to find them, refine them, and make it easier for experts and novices to follow them.

At the same time, we obviously can't rely on shadow learning as some kind of new normal. One, it's not right. Up close, all these practices would make us wince. Experts and the public have settled on current techniques and standards, and they're not just comforting window dressing. Mostly they protect us and represent reasoned approaches to complex problems. Violating these willy-nilly is a nonstarter. On top of that, no one should have to risk getting fired—or harming a patient—just to master their job. We need to find ways of building skill that increase our respect and trust for one another while facilitating sharing of expertise and collaboration. Relying on counternormative tactics will do the opposite: breed inequality and mistrust, hiding and isolation. Appropriateness aside, shadow learning is not universally effective, nor is it practical for most people: it worked for some of those I've studied, but remember, they were rare. Those one in eight residents who found their way to a shadow learning path were at top teaching hospitals. The rest struggled, failed to learn well, yet were legally empowered to do robotic surgery. And we shouldn't accept one-in-ten odds that an inverted apprenticeship will work out well for skill. Most novices would end up on the short end of the skill stick, with a lower-quality job experience to boot. So while we have to find it and study it, we shouldn't treat it as gospel.

So, there's a dynamic universe of shadow learning out there, and in important ways this book aims a telescope at just a few patches of that night sky. That means understanding shadow learning more thoroughly is job number one. Practices like the ones I've uncovered are hard-won, tested paths in a hyperspeed digital world where gaining expertise alongside intelligent tech is becoming more difficult, more important, and more urgent. Shadow learners offer critical clues about the path forward for every organization, every profession, and every person. We need to learn from them, so we can revive healthy challenge, complexity, and connection for the rest of us. In the next chapter I've pulled together key principles and tactics to help us get started; let's turn to reworking the skill code, together.

CHAPTER SEVEN

REWORKING THE SKILL CODE

Ernie trudges down an abandoned, sandy road in the midday sun, with a 109-degree breeze at his back. It's just another day at the office: he's off to defuse a bomb.

He's wearing a seventy-five-pound protective suit and shrapnel-proof helmet, both made of thick layers of Kevlar and plastic, all coated with fire-retardant materials. His hands, however, are exposed to the breeze, fingers flicking through rehearsed disarmament techniques as he makes his way toward his target. All he can hear is the crunch of the gravel and the sound of his own breath in his mask. As he gets close to his target—in this case a tattered Pokémon backpack near a schoolyard—his vision sharpens up and he scans the area for disturbances or wires. Step by step, he works his way closer to the device. He reports via his headset in spare, dry language that he's about to move in. By the book, step by step, he works his way closer to this device. He takes a knee, a deep breath, and reaches for his tools: it's go time.

Before robots entered the picture, the task looked a lot like I've just described here: you dealt with an improvised explosive device (IED) by walking up to it and going through a set of procedures. Where's the novice in this picture? A hundred meters away in a bomb-proof truck. Hard for them to learn from Ernie while he's working: by protocol, he's not all that chatty, especially because they don't know how long they have. The bomb could go off, and so could the locals. Even if he could talk more, there's only so much information he could convey about what he was seeing, his assessment and decision making, and his technique. And they only have one shot at the problem. Of course, after-action reviews help a bit, but hands-on training was a serious bottleneck. Ernie remembered the old pain of being a novice all too well—it felt like breathing through a straw.

To be a specialist in explosive ordnance disposal (EOD) takes more than a year of intensive training and is one of the most dangerous and prestigious positions in the military. It also happens to be one of the only jobs that I have come across where the use of robots didn't block skill development but enhanced it.

In 2001 the PackBot arrived for military duty.[1] This forty-pound, tanklike, one-armed robot was built by the same MIT-connected engineering team that gave us the Roomba (yes, the household vacuuming robot). It entered military service in 2002 and opened up new possibilities for EOD almost immediately.[2] After an initial period of experimentation and design changes, a new work pattern emerged that took advantage of the technology's capabilities.

Now Ernie sits side by side with his trainee Deshaun in the same bomb-proof truck, and Ernie guides him through the procedure of approaching the bomb. Deshaun is the one in physical control, not Ernie, using a controller that looks remarkably similar to Deshaun's PlayStation back home. That frees Ernie up to focus on situational awareness and tactics to prompt Deshaun with questions to develop the same skill. They still have to work briskly, but their side-by-side interactions have a lot more give-and-take where there was virtually none before. The introduction of the PackBot made it a lot easier for Deshaun to learn from Ernie on the job.

Right now, the positive outcome with bomb disposal is the exception to the rule. The stark picture in the last chapter is clear: the way we're handling most intelligent technologies blocks healthy challenge, complexity, and connection, instead of enhancing them. On average, we've started a war between technological productivity and human skill, and skill is losing. Going back to good old-fashioned apprenticeships isn't often a good option in our increasingly hybrid, digital, and fragmented workplaces. But if we continue to undermine healthy challenge, complexity, and connection and sever the traditional expert-novice bond with no new one in place, we're going to find ourselves in a world of trouble.

That's why it's important to rework the skill code. First, we need to learn which sequences and approaches to challenge, complexity, and connection are working, and how they're different from the status quo. We also need to be putting these skill-related innovations into practice—changing techniques, technologies, work systems, and even organizations. If we do this, we can do far more to preserve its vital role as the world changes. With a reworked skill code in hand, we can put it straight to work, no matter what technology you're dealing with. Why? Not a one of the three Cs says anything about technology. They're technology agnostic. That means we don't have to give up new technologies or productivity gains to preserve healthy challenge, complexity, and connection, and we shouldn't: the path to a healthy future requires them all. In fact—and this is key—there are probably many cases where insisting on both productivity and skill will get us better outcomes in both categories than we would otherwise.

The PackBot itself is not the point. We can't solve our skill problems by building robots just like the PackBot for each industry. The robot design was only part of what made the novice-expert relationship work so well. The controller could just as easily have ended up in Ernie's hands, with Deshaun looking on, trying to work his way into the action—saving the day, perhaps, but killing skill development in the process. What matters most—but is too often missing when we adopt gee-whiz tech—is how that tool will be used, and whether that will enhance skill for a novice. Some of that is shaped by design, but a lot of it is down to implementation. In fact, there might well be times where the senior EOD tech *does* take control too frequently. But overall, someone, somewhere, decided that the trainee would take primary physical control. We need to begin our journey to save our skill right at that moment, because that's where the power is. Right here, right now, we can take control of the way we're designing and using technology, so we get results and improve healthy challenge, complexity, and connection at the same time.

Thankfully, we have a wealth of field-tested guidance from shadow learning that might help us resolve this dilemma. Some of those off-the-map, deviant tactics that risk catastrophe and punishment offer a glimmer of how we could change work to preserve skill, even as we use our latest technologies. Staying after hours in a "closed" hospice care ward protects healthy challenge for a new nurse. Skipping shifts to watch a maintenance tech ensures healthy complexity for a heavy construction equipment operator. Skimming case reviews saves the time to buy a coffee for the defense counsel, which builds healthy connection for a junior lawyer. These determined innovators show us new ways to ensure the health of the three essential components needed to build skill in a changing world. How can we leverage these insights at scale?

We can't be naïve: it won't always be possible to protect the skill code and productivity. Sometimes profit from automation will be so significant that it's not feasible or appropriate to also insist on skill development in the work that remains. Once roofers got nail guns, it often wasn't profitable to let them do the more challenging, complex work of swinging hammers anymore. When email arrived, typing a letter and putting it in the mail often seemed pointless. It likewise won't always be wise to scale shadow learning. Some of its lessons will be flawed or incomplete and will lead us down costly blind alleys. Remember, most inverted apprenticeships left novices overwhelmed and underskilled, while only barely improving experts' skill. But the skill code can and will need to survive and thrive in the face of a potential breakdown of our adaptability as a species, not to mention a lot of the meaning we derive from work. And just as in our rearview mirrors, these threats may be closer than they appear: GPT-style technology has been adopted far faster by far more people than any automating technology in history. And it's not alone—hold on to your hats for a wild tour of additional, massive technological disruptions in the next chapter. If we're going to take a stand for human skill, the time is right now, and we've got to give it everything we've got.

THREE KEYS TO REWORKING THE SKILL CODE: DISCOVER, DEVELOP, AND DEPLOY

To revive and maintain the three Cs—healthy challenge, complexity, and connection in our work—we need general guidelines that will help make skill a consequence, not a casualty as we drive new technology into fields and professions around the globe.

A healthy set of guidelines isn't far away—all we have to do is shift from the three Cs to the three Ds, a set of mutually reinforcing activities that nurture human skill and adaptability: discover, develop, and deploy. First and foremost, we have to *discover* the specific approaches that preserve the health of the skill code in our contexts—whether that's a team, an organization, a profession, or an industry. Then we need to *develop* organizations and technologies that foster both productivity and healthy challenge, complexity, and connection. Robotic bomb disposal turned out better for skill building than robotic surgery, and that was driven by the features engineers used when they were working together, and the processes developed in the organizations that purchased these technologies. Finally, we have to consider how we *deploy* technology: how we alter various work processes, who we involve in that, and how we configure technologies to suit. Any solution has to address both the technical and the social sides of the ledger if we're going to preserve skill while securing the productivity boons promised by new technology. If we do that, not only will we have a skills solution, but it will be self-improving, because we've repaired the learning mechanism at its core.

DISCOVER

Discovery is where to begin: we need to build deeper understanding of the skill code and shadow learning that sit at the core of this book. We need to do this ASAP, before the technology that's dismantling the skill code also drives shadow learners deeper underground, into more secluded, unregulated places.

Assuming we have complete—or even near-complete—understanding of the problem is a recipe for wasted effort and potential failure. For example, we now have the skill code—the building blocks of skill development, for humans and perhaps even AI. We have checklists for healthy challenge, complexity, and connection. Under the hood, it is these more atomic aspects of skill development that traditional expert-novice collaboration promotes so seamlessly, and what shadow learners have sought out in new and risky ways. All that insight is critical and useful right away, but it is also just the beginning: the alphabet and a few stock phrases in the language of skill development. Now it's time to learn how to speak that language in a way that makes sense to the locals where *you* live: your team, your organization, your profession, and your industry.

That means most discovery is local, so we need your help. What combinations work best? When do challenge and complexity go together better than challenge and connection? What about sequences? When is it better to emphasize complexity before challenge? Why? While we'll learn some general principles here, there's probably no abstract answer to these questions that works equally well in all settings. How does the answer to those questions change when we're talking about different skills, whether it is how to tie a surgical knot, code a website, or comfort an autistic child, for example?

How is the threat to skill showing up where you are? How do healthy challenge, complexity, and connection show up in contexts that matter to you? Where are they under threat, and how, specifically? On both fronts: Why? If you want to improve the skill situation for you and your coworkers, you need these specifics to inspire and inform the collective action required for change. When it comes to progress, there's usually a handshake between hifalutin ideas (often found in books like this) and local know-how and motivation. In 1995, John Kotter, the Harvard researcher focused on organizational change, gave us a clear set of findings that have stood the test of time: until you can hold up real, locally credible examples of a problem to your collaborators, they won't see the threat and won't make the investments and sacrifices required to improve the situation.[3] The threat to skill and the skill code are no exception. And you can find those examples. Each of us has to invest precious time and resources looking into these questions if we want to improve skill development for ourselves and those we care about.

In fact, whenever we're not in discovery mode, we're running blind into our work, our organizations, and the next century. The further we run like that, the less our old approaches to skill will serve us. A policy for certifying environmental toxicologists might block potentially risky task performance while working remote at a cleanup site. A serious blow to healthy challenge. A job rotation system in finance might fail because it doesn't take new, cross-departmental workflows into account. Healthy complexity is off the table. An apprenticeship for nursing may founder, given that so many jump departments, hospitals, and even geographic regions so frequently now. Healthy connection just wouldn't be there. Finding all this out takes discovery work, and because the problem is specific to your context, nobody else can handle it but you. The problem is also dynamic—we regularly create new tools, techniques, and ways of organizing effort. So, while an initial burst of discovery work may be critical, we have to keep at it, or else we'll slide out of touch again. Refreshing your understanding of the skill code—and the dynamics that underlie it—gives you clear tactics to keep this bond healthy and the skill flowing.

Along the same lines, you need solid information about the solution already in motion: there's a dynamic universe of shadow learning out there, and in important ways this book just opens the discussion. That means understanding shadow learning more thoroughly is also job number one. Everything in chapter 6 is powerful guidance in the middle of a global threat to skill. At the same time, there's simply no way it's an exhaustive accounting of the useful shadow learning out there, let alone its unintended negative side effects or its useful reapplication for most experts and novices. Our mandate for ongoing discovery work is just as strong—if not stronger—here as it is with uncovering blocks to the healthy challenge, complexity, and connection necessary for skill development.

There's also a deeper reason discovery is critical when it comes to shadow learning: it's liable to get "darker"—less ethical and more hidden. Why? It's getting harder to find a "forgiveness rather than permission" zone where you can bend rules and break with convention to find a new way. We've wired up the globe with an interconnected system of cheap sensors—keyboards, touchscreens, cameras, GPS chips, fingerprint scanners, networks to transmit and store the data, and now, crucially, machine-learning algorithms to analyze and make predictions based on this data. Each year that we build out this infrastructure it gets radically easier to observe, analyze, judge, and control individual behavior—not just as workers but also as citizens. Who gets to decide whether a professor is pacing her lectures appropriately, or whether a beat cop is taking too long to report back as they reach their patrol destinations? Or whether any of us was adapting or innovating appropriately? Ten years ago, the answer was basically one person. Now it can be many, including those who have access off-site and after the fact. Anyone can call foul, and all of them are empowered with massive new sources of rich data and predictive analytics. All this means that the gray area for benign shadow learning is shrinking. Few people prefer to innovate and adapt in ways that risk catastrophe or punishment—but some will turn in this direction when they know that approved means will fail. Like it or not, more and more critical skill development will be happening in areas of social life previously reserved for "capital-*D*" deviants, criminals, and ne'er-do-wells.

Not a pleasant picture, but probably an accurate one. Leaders, organizations, groups, and individuals that can learn from shadow learners in their context will get ahead.

One approach I've seen work is to cultivate an organizational culture of psychological safety: one where people are more willing to share their shadow learning because they trust they won't pay a price for it. But even if you make it your life's work, you can't afford to wait for psychological safety to kick in, or to bet the farm on it. You need insight into the shadows *now*. You can complement the "change from within" approach above by securing "eyes from without." Specifically, you can bring in a neutral third party who can ensure strict anonymity while uncovering and comparing shadow learning practices across diverse cases. The key here is that this individual should be deeply trusted, so normal consultants working for executives may not cut it. The people I was studying came to know and trust me: they were aware that I was observing work in numerous work groups and facilities, that they could decline to participate at any time, and that I would never share data that could be attributed to them, their colleagues, or their organization. I don't think they would have opened up otherwise. Another way to get this kind of insight is to visit other contexts that do work like your home base, but again you'd have to do this in a way that made it clear that anyone talking to you or being observed had strong protections from being revealed. These approaches could help you do the same in your context.

But from here on in, you're the expert: You know your own context and its social dynamics. You know trusted people inside and outside of your organization who can help flesh out the picture. You might even have creative, shadowy solutions of your own. No one can tell you how to unearth shadow learning tactics in your context without this kind of insider knowledge. They wouldn't know who to ask, what to ask, what to look for, and what to be sensitive about. You know enough to get started. So, it's up to you to get to work discovering it all.

DEVELOP

If we stopped with discovery, this would be a play-from-the-sidelines event, and we need intervention and results if we're going to bend the arc of history in our favor. The first step? We need to develop new rules for the skill development game before stepping on the field.

This begins with "simple" (that is to say, fiendishly complicated, risky, and uncertain) changes in our normal routines. The way we've been handling technology has gotten us where we are. We've been designing and selling it to extend experts' capabilities. We've been putting it to work for that purpose. And we've been sacrificing novice involvement in the process. If that's all you knew, you'd be faced with many difficult decisions about using technology. A "yes" vote would mean sacrificing skill for productivity, and a "no" would mean the opposite. Not the kind of solution that most of us would contemplate for long.

But you have the skill code in your hands now, and with each successive C, you've been accumulating a quiverful of microtactics that are implementable most anywhere, anytime. It doesn't matter what kind of technology you're dealing with, what the work process is, who is involved, and so on. The basic move is to consider the situation and ask how you could ensure healthy challenge, complexity, and connection while also getting significant benefit from the technology at hand. To up the ante, you might even look for ways that insisting on the skill code could deliver higher productivity.

Here are a few ideas that can get you started, but at a high level: ease up on control, relax hierarchy and status, and just follow the skill.

Realign Roles

Remember those investment bankers in chapter 6? As it became apparent that "best practice" was for junior bankers to run software queries and to hand these off to senior bankers who would work alone on deals, one of the groups developed an alternative work arrangement. Junior analysts continued to pull raw reports to produce the needed input, but they worked alongside senior partners on the analysis that followed. This group realigned job roles to reconnect experts and novices.

In some ways this was a risky business move, though. It slowed down the process, and because it required the junior analysts to handle a wider range of valuation methods and calculations at a breakneck pace, it introduced mistakes that were difficult to catch. But the junior analysts developed a deeper knowledge of the multiple companies and other stakeholders involved in an M&A and of the relevant industry and built skill required to manage the entire valuation process. Rather than function as a cog in a system they didn't understand, they engaged in the broader complexity of the work and built bonds with senior bankers—all of that positioned them to take on more-senior roles. Another benefit was that the junior and senior bankers discovered that, far from being interchangeable, the software packages they'd been using to create inputs for analysis sometimes produced valuations of a given company that were billions of dollars apart.[4] Had junior analysts remained siloed from their senior managers, that might never have come to light. These teams of shadow learners may have paid a short-term price for inefficiency, but they built skill, increased their meaning and connection to the work itself, and even found an existential analytical threat in the process. Not a bad deal.

This skill-enhancing innovation wasn't exactly planned, and it certainly wasn't informed by an understanding of the skill code. So, you can do much better. Finding out what to change isn't as easy as examining job descriptions, unfortunately. Experts and novices will often get pulled apart in practice, but are technically still performing the same tasks, so job descriptions don't change. Senior surgeons' and residents' formal responsibilities didn't change to reflect the brutal disconnect that I found in my research, for example. If you're dealing with a larger organization, the richness of their interaction might show up in other places, though, like how much time people with expert- and novice-level titles spend in the same rooms or how many calendar invites include people in both roles. If those numbers have crept downward, you could mandate they go up to a certain threshold to align expert and novice roles in a coarse way. For surgery this could be as simple as the amount of time residents spent in the OR. Or for a more targeted approach, you can realign roles related to a critical joint work product. In the case of my surgical research? You could measure resident control time on the console—not time in the OR—and lean on attendings to grant more control. I can almost guarantee this will be easier in your case than in mine because the new surgical robot made residents *completely* optional, and life was on the line. In most cases, decreased novice participation is a matter of degree, and outcomes are less intense. But the basic questions apply in both cases: Where have experts and novices gotten practically separated in ways that hurt challenge, complexity, and connection, and how can you realign their roles to address that—while preserving productivity gains?

Rework Your Metrics

That previous example shows that there's all kinds of data you can collect related to the checklists underlying the skill code, and that you can use this new data to motivate and focus yourself, your team, and your organization. To learn a powerful lesson about changes in metrics, let's return to Sarah Brayne's study of the Los Angeles Police Department after they'd implemented PredPol, a predictive policing system that sent cops to strange areas of the city based on prior data. When beat cops had trouble integrating predictive analytics into their work, some police chiefs reframed expectations for them. Brayne found that many officers assigned to patrol AI-designated routes appeared to be less productive on traditional measures such as number of arrests, citations, and FIs (field interview cards—records made by officers of their contacts with citizens, typically people who seem suspicious). FIs are particularly important in AI-assisted policing because they provide crucial input data for predictive systems even when no arrests result. When cops went where the system directed them, they often made no arrests, wrote no tickets, and created no FIs: there was nothing suspicious going on there! According to the algorithm, they were being sent to places where crime *would* happen. Cops did *not* like this, even if it deterred crime. They were bred for *action*, whether that was talking to potential suspects or exploring a crime scene. And their performance measurement system counted FIs, not crimes-that-might-have-happened. They looked bad.

Recognizing that these traditional measures discouraged beat cops from following the system's recommendations, a few chiefs sidestepped standard practice and publicly and privately praised officers not for making arrests and delivering citations but for learning to work with the algorithmic assignments. As one captain said, "Good, fine, but we are telling you where the probability of a crime is at, so sit there, and if you come in with a zero [no crimes], that is a success." These chiefs were taking a risk by encouraging what many saw as bad policing, but in doing so they were helping to move the law enforcement culture toward a future in which the police will increasingly collaborate with intelligent machines, whether or not that particular AI remains in the tool kit.

Your knowledge of the skill code means you could go much, much further than this accidental discovery. What specific tactics in chapters 2 through 4 are particularly helpful—or rare—in your context, and how could you measure and reward those in conjunction with typical performance metrics? Remember, for example, that recovering from minor mistakes is a critical part of healthy challenge. How could you measure and *reward* that? In Casey's world—the postsurgical ICU—she and the attending physician could unearth, count, and highlight Casey's minor overnight mistakes during morning rounds the next day. Where did she administer too much or too little medication or fluids, and how did she notice the problem and correct it? And what about mistakes of omission: Where she didn't intubate a patient, but should have? And how did she notice and recover from that one? They could start tracking, counting, and quantifying this activity, and using it as a benchmark for how well the residency was going. Clinical leaders could also expand this from a one-off success to an organizational asset by turning it into part of a performance metric. If you ran critical care for this hospital, you could have your IT group add a short set of "difficulty recovery" fields to the morning rounds note-taking app, and critical care docs could then run reports on this to highlight and celebrate this critical part of the skill development process. Whether you're working at the individual, hyperlocal level or you have far-reaching control over organization design and infrastructure, you can convert traditional performance measurement systems into an ally in the quest for skill: What could you count and set goals around that would nudge people toward healthy challenge, complexity, and connection?

Tap Frontline Know-how

Let's revisit the powerful example set by inverted apprenticeships. When new technologies arrive, experts will struggle to learn— they're hyperfocused on the "hard" parts of problems, so they lose a holistic sense of the work and they often can't find the time or even allow themselves to appear to be novices, given their status. So, they build new skills by mooching off the newbies who do see the whole picture and have the skill or are supposed to build it anyway. Why not formally tap that know-how? Create opportunities for novices to experiment with new technologies, then put *them* in a formal training or coaching role. That formality will help experts save face where they might otherwise be concerned about looking incompetent.

Inverted apprenticeships aren't the only solution, of course. Why not move people around to take on new and different tasks and expose them to new information? For some, this will foster deep expertise, but it won't much correspond to their job title. In surgery, for example, senior docs got hyperfocused on the innards of a patient and lost touch with the bigger picture of how a procedure runs. To understand this, residents sometimes turned to scrub techs, the lowest workers on the totem pole in the OR, who saw the procedure in its totality: the patient's entire body; the position and movement of the robot's arms; the activities of the anesthesiologist, the nurse, and others around the patient; and all the instruments and supplies from start to finish. The best scrubs have paid careful attention during thousands of procedures. When residents shift from the console to the bedside, therefore, some bypassed the attending physician and went straight to these "superscrubs" with technical questions, such as whether the intra-abdominal pressure is unusual, or when to clear the field of fluid or of smoke from cauterization. They do this despite norms and often unbeknownst to the attending.

There's nothing necessarily shady about tapping frontline know-how. If you're a leader, you can create new, prestigious jobs for your sharpest workers so they can serve as instructors and coaches. What if "superscrub" were a real title? What if residents had to do a two-week rotation with *them,* and you gave those scrubs training in how to coach those residents? A dose of humility for the residents, a status and pay bump for the scrubs, but also a skills bump for both parties. And you could tap their expertise outside the confines of a live procedure: when it came time to do an OR redesign, to invest in new technology or rework materials handling from central supply and cleaning services, you could invite them to that process. Whether it's in midwifery, acting and film production, hospitality, or firefighting, new technology means you've got new experts peppered in the organization around you, and everyone can win if you formalize that. Or if we're just talking about your personal skills journey and you don't have power to reorganize the work or allocate financial resources, look around you for where the *actual* expertise lies that you're after, and formally arrange to connect with that person as a mentor. Forget whether they're younger than you. Get paid less or more than you. Get over it and set up an inverted apprenticeship: they're the expert and you're the novice, period.

Exercise Surveillance Restraint

Improving without data is hard. Sometimes impossible. And new forms of data and analysis can offer dramatic improvements—remember how long checkout lines took before laser scanners? It's essential that we experiment with new kinds of data and analytics to assess their value.

At the same time, sometimes your organization, team, or even a single coworker will build more skill if you leave stones unturned and cameras off. To take just a tiny step in this direction in a robotic surgery, this might mean turning off the TVs while a resident is operating. Then only their mentor could see what they're doing. You might want to do this kind of thing earlier on in residents' training to give them space to make minor mistakes and to struggle without the entire room coming to a snap judgment about their capability. It's that kind of early judgment that leads residents to conclude they have to build skill away from prying eyes.

At a certain point, surveillance, analysis, prediction, and control stop yielding returns: not because the data or predictions are wrong, but because you are destroying the underobserved and informal spaces where people feel free to experiment, fail, and think through a problem. Workers will stop messing around with scrap materials at a construction site after hours. Scientists will avoid personal experiments on expensive lab equipment that logs each use with a user ID. Teachers will leave their lesson plans alone if an administrator's watching for changes. Moreover, excessive surveillance, quantification, and predictive analytics can drive the work experience down the toilet. Knowing that we're being overly surveilled, measured, and judged by a remote "other" shoots a hole in these critical sources of intrinsic motivation and work satisfaction. Only a shortsighted organization would be willing to sacrifice these for the sake of just one more layer of insight. Always, the question should be: What's the *least* we could measure to get great productivity and skill?

Knowing where the line is—where beneficial collection and analysis stop and the dysfunction starts—will be exceptionally difficult in cultures or organizations that prize technical progress and data-based decision making. So, ironically, it may be companies like Facebook, Amazon, Google, and Apple that struggle the most here. Because it's hard to get good data on the subtler, negative side effects and easier to get data on the short-run, positive effects, you'll need strong leadership to investigate whether technical infrastructure like cameras or keystroke-tracking software are doing more harm than good. In regulation-heavy, surveillance-resistant places like Europe, all of this will probably be easier, while testing and adopting new tools will be harder. Regardless, announcing a reasoned choice to exercise surveillance restraint and the rationale for it makes leadership accountable, and it can increase trust and encourage inventive skill building closer to the light of day.

They say an ounce of prevention is worth a pound of cure. That's certainly the driving force behind this section. We need to draw on the skill code to develop a system of durable organizational structures like policies, norms, rules, processes, and roles that will help *anyone* build skill as they do their job. But for every aphorism there's an equal and opposite counter-aphorism. In this case, it's Mike Tyson's famous "everyone's got a plan until they get punched in the face." Our best-laid plans, processes, and infrastructure are simply no match for the surprises that come in the tussle of everyday work. That's why we also have to focus on the doing.

DEPLOY

Across eighteen of the top teaching hospitals in the US, all the clinical leaders I interviewed agreed that involving residents more in procedures would be incredibly beneficial but were concerned about laying down policy to make it so. A chair of urology gave it to me straight: "How as a department chair do you go to [top surgeons] and say, 'Hey, you guys are not teaching, you gotta let them do more surgery.' And they say, 'Well, what if they fuck up my patients? I can't do that.' I don't have the right then to say, 'You must do it.' Because they have a patient to worry about, and they got malpractice to worry about, and they have outcomes to worry about."

I'm going to tell you a secret about the robot my surgeons used, one that could have unlocked new solutions to this problem, and that many robotic surgeons themselves don't know: two people can share simultaneous control of a single robot—one from a standard console and one from a "teaching" console. In principle, this was designed to allow for "driver's ed"–style education—the attending can use the brakes while the resident steers and uses the gas. But I never observed this, the attendings and residents I studied said they never saw it, and salespeople told me the practice was exceptionally rare. At these top-tier hospitals, the second set of controls was a running joke among residents: many called it the "napping" console.

This is the impact of poor deployment choices. Many hospitals bought this surgical robot that had two consoles—one for an expert and one for a novice. And, it turns out, it had a special feature to allow for even finer-grained sharing of control to allow experts to better mentor those novices. But if you don't put all this to use in the heat of the moment, when there are real trade-offs to be made, it's all just an academic exercise. At *teaching* hospitals? All that awareness of a problem, all that advanced surgical robotic technology designed for learning, and . . . nothing happened. Skill was dying. And in many cases, that's not the worst of it: everyone—residents, attendings, administrators, potential recruits—got their hopes up about skill building, only to have them dashed and their morale sapped. That can be worse than doing nothing.

Deployment is when your plan makes contact with reality, and where you have to take a stand for skill.

To get started—whether you're working virtually, in person, or in a hybrid setting—assume you can get productivity out of technology and amplify skill in using it. If you've done a lot of discovery work and have developed excellent processes to support skill development, this will be easier, both mentally and practically. But it's still possible in conditions quite hostile to skill. The main difference will be the size of the lump in your throat: some people will not be expecting or support this line of inquiry and may have an interest in preserving the productivity-obsessed status quo. No matter what role we're in—a leader, making technology and organizational change decisions; a technologist, building and marketing intelligent technologies; a venture capitalist, choosing which technologies to support; or a frontline worker, having to deal with intelligent technologies every day—we can all help by asking the same question: How can we handle this technology in a way that gets results and builds capability in the people using it? If we want to preserve our most powerful way of building valuable skill, we need to insist on solutions that achieve both goals at the same time. This won't always be possible, but we won't know until we try.

If you were a resident and you walked into a normal robotic surgical training program, you could ask your attending this question. They'd probably be aware that standard operating procedure would cut you out of the action. And they probably wouldn't have much of an idea about how to solve the problem. Ask anyway and do your best to come with a creative solution in mind. If you knew the robotic secret I revealed above, you could of course suggest that you two work out a few new tactics to take advantage of the driver's ed features. The attending would build new skills and so would you: they would learn how to scaffold your learning via shared control of a robot, and you would get scaffolded into more complex and challenging territory than you could handle on your own. And you'd be building healthy connection, too. Maybe you could even write up a paper about what you learned, to spread the word.

If you're the attending or the chief of urology in this scenario, you have different options. You can turn to the technology vendor and ask them for lessons learned about how surgeons share control most productively with residents. You're asking for *their* discovery and development work. Ask them how you and your organization could be a place to prove there's a better way to use the technology, when it comes to the skill code. Give them this book and tell them to come back with a list of features and techniques with their technology that they believe could support healthy challenge, complexity, and connection. They might look at you like you had two heads at first. That's okay. It's an unusual request in a world that so blindly throws skill under the bus on the warpath to productivity. Let them squirm for a week or so. They'll come up with something, and here something's definitely better than nothing.

If you're the technologist in this picture, you have a huge market opportunity. Your competitors do *not* have this issue on their radar. Even if they did—the maker of the surgical robot I studied was clearly aware of it to some degree—they probably don't have a good working theory of skill, so their new features or recommended deployment strategies will fall flat. Yours won't. You can emphasize features of your technology that subtly nudge your users to preserve healthy challenge, complexity, and connection, even as they get great results with it. Maybe you have an offline app. Maybe mention that users can take it home with them to reflect more effectively on the complexity of the work they just dealt with that day. Or maybe remind your customers that their users can look at your stats dashboard to see other users who are at comparable spots in their skill development, so they can connect with each other more effectively. In the case of the surgical robot I studied, how about suggesting attendings turn on the timer feature so they can see it's been ten minutes since they last handed the resident the controls? Or make it a point to tell the department chair that they can get "sharing" statistics—so she can tell which attendings are giving residents the most uninterrupted time in direct control. If you take a fresh look at your feature set and standard best practices, you can find items like this, and you can claim brand value by being the "skill-centric" automation provider in your market.

Of course, all these deployment tactics are not a stand-alone. You don't want to be in a position of constantly having to save the day when it comes to skill. But as a complement to good discovery and development work, they are an absolute necessity. All of us need to cultivate the skill, knowledge, and values required to defend healthy challenge, complexity, and connection as our days roll by. If we are going to keep our meta superpower—the ability to build skill while we work—we have to start somewhere, because we know that intelligent technologies are becoming exponentially more capable, and employers are incorporating them into workplaces more and more with each passing day. We know that organizations often handle intelligent machines in ways that make it easier for a single expert to take more control of the work, reducing dependence on trainees' help. Robotic systems allow senior surgeons to operate with less assistance, so they do. Investment banking systems allow senior partners to exclude junior analysts from complex valuations, so they do. Everyone should insist on discovery, development, and deployment work that improves productivity but also supports work involving healthy challenge, complexity, and connection.

These three Ds are a powerful set of tools to begin setting things right. But they are only a beginning: they are about finding ways through a system that privileges efficiency over learning, because we're handling increasingly intelligent technologies in a way that blocks healthy challenge, complexity, and connection. They take a slow-changing system for granted—all its technologies, all its norms, all its techniques and processes are the headwind, and the three Ds are a new set of sails.

We need to be bolder than that. To flourish in a world that will continue changing even as we discover, develop, and deploy new methods, we need to think beyond the notion that technology is an enemy of skill. We need to envision how technology could be skill's ally.

If it hadn't occurred to you already, then you're in for a pleasant surprise: AI, robotics, and intelligent technologies could enable a new, beating heart of skill development around the globe, enriching billions of lives and extending our already wondrous capabilities so we can meet the challenges in front of us. And whether he said it or not, that quote attributed to William Gibson is right again on this issue: this is already happening in fits and starts in isolated pockets of our global economy. So, let's turn from the present to the future and start to imagine what our world could be like if we augmented skill development with the very technologies we're concerned about. One where just using our technologies built our skill. What would that look like?

CHAPTER EIGHT

SKILL'S CHIMERIC FUTURE

I t's 2037, and Sara is a journeyman welder in a high-end custom shop in Erie, Pennsylvania. She has a problem: a client from Cornell University wants her to help them build most of a custom quantum computing rig. Ever since that 2029 breakthrough in quantum computing substrates out at the University of California, Santa Barbara, this hyperfuturistic, almost fictional technology became far more practical than anyone expected—far more quickly, too. A rig like the one she's been tasked to build works about 158 million times faster than a classical supercomputer—taking four minutes to complete a computation that would otherwise take ten thousand years. That's not what's got her attention, though. She's focused on how to get the job done. A lot of the work she knows how to do, but their design requires significant plastic welding—joining multiple 3D-printed plastic components together with an ultrasonic tool. She's never done this before, and her boss and crew haven't, either. Naturally, she takes the gig.

Sara knows she has two weeks to get up to speed—that's the lead time for the device and the materials—and she's confident that she'll be ready by then. That afternoon, she dons her augmented reality (or AR) headset and logs in to SkillNet: a global, AI-enabled, crowd-curated platform for skill development across a wide range of occupations and skill levels. A quick, immersive run-through of the basics in ultrasonic welding awaits her, but SkillNet's power runs far deeper: its AI had recommended she take this gig in the first place. Based on fine-grained, rich data on all her past work—every job, all the tools she'd used, all her client and internal communications, all her motion as she did the work—the system told her that this order would be challenging, but achievable, and that she'd find it an interesting complement to the aluminum work she normally did. Tim, her boss, had also given it a thumbs-up, and said he'd shadow her when he could and would watch for SkillNet notifications that his guidance might be helpful. She activates the run-through, a digital ultrasonic welding rig appears on her real work bench, and she gets a simple verbal invitation: "go ahead—turn it on." Sara has no idea where the right button is, but she smiles, and tries one that looks right: she is excited to get learning.

By the time the welder and materials had arrived, Sara had ten increasingly difficult hours of practice under her belt (and the regional high score on the final simulation, thank you very much), a certificate of completion on her SkillNet profile for an introductory ultrasonics practicum, and a message from her client, praising her initiative and progress. And two days earlier, SkillNet had suggested a few experts as live mentors for her during the work—highly rated experts outside Sara's organization whose skill and style were a good match for her and the project. Sara chose Rizky, an Indonesian ultrasonics whiz—beyond all the work stuff, her brother-in-law was Indonesian, too, so she knew they'd also probably have Nasi Goreng recipes to chat about. SkillNet booked their first work session. Sara then reviewed a SkillNet-generated supercut of Rizky's last few jobs, responded to its prompts to identify what was going on in various clips for Rizky to review, then she went home for the weekend. She was ready.

Sara's first day is a blast. She puts on her AR welding glasses and gloves, and Rizky's avatar and tools appear in her workspace. Sara also notices that a few novice welders—and even a high school student and a retiree—had requested observational access. She accepts them all, then starts the session. Live translated from Indonesian, Rizky walks Sara through the initial setup with the tool—it's a lot like normal welding, so this goes fast—and she sets to doing a few practice welds on some dummy materials. Rizky watches as Sara tries, giving her verbal and visual guidance as she goes, and per Sara's previous settings, SkillNet grants her "recovery points" as she addresses minor mistakes. Once the practice is through, Sara gets out the quantum data plane so she can join it to the control and measurement planes, and SkillNet subtly blurs out the proprietary components and details of the job for Rizky and the observers to protect Sara's client. Rizky coaches her on the subtleties of joining these composite materials, and Sara's gloves give her physical feedback to guide her toward applying the right forces in the right way. When they're both satisfied Sara can handle the work, Sara thanks Rizky. They both answer observer and SkillNet questions for fifteen minutes, then upload their session to SkillNet. Sara uploads her subsequent work there, too, knowing that she'll receive a raft of feedback and questions from the SkillNet AI and welders around the planet. She looks forward to offering the same in return to new aluminum welders out there. Sara's also proud that she learned a new skill in such a short time, and excited to get to work on this cutting-edge project.

In a moment of reflection, Sara shakes her head in wonder. She's thirty-seven. She started welding thirteen years ago in 2024, and none of this would have been possible. She was lucky if she could find a half-decent clip on YouTube after a few hours of searching.

As if that was really going to help her get ahead. Now? Her ultra-sonics skill journey is on rocket fuel. Challenge? Check: she's taking on a project far outside her prior skill set, and she's scaffolded through increasingly difficult tasks and minor failures that she couldn't handle on her own. Complexity? Check: she's dealing with new tools, new processes, new materials, and a new work product, all of which involve different dynamics, but are connected to her prior work in interesting ways. Connection? Check: she and Rizky chose to work together, they now have a warm bond of trust and respect, and she's got Rizky's public endorsement for more work of this kind. And she's not the only one who benefits. Rizky? He's got the satisfaction of paying it forward, gotten a few refreshers on aluminum and some SkillNet-generated tips on his coaching, and has earned more respect from the global welding community. Those truly novice welders? They got a detailed look at a corner of their profession that they might not have known much about—real problems and expert-novice coaching interactions included. The high school student and retiree got a deep, fascinating dive on cutting-edge, expert work. Certainly, some newfound respect for the welding occupation, and who knows, this might tip them into getting more involved.

Sara's scenario is a little futuristic but requires no fiction. It takes currently available technology, presumes it will become more cost effective by 2037, and blends the cheaper, better versions together for the sake of skill development in the flow of natural work. In 2024, we have high-quality AR: Apple's just announced their $3,500 headset.[1] Meta has their rough equivalent.[2] Both blend digital and physical reality. We have ChatGPT and its analogues that—if artfully prompted—can serve as coaches. And Microsoft and Google have both announced that their GPT-enabled systems will be able to make custom content creation recommendations for you based on your "knowledge graph"—all your prior emails, IMs, photos, documents, and so on.[3] And we have online platforms like GitHub,* YouTube, and Reddit for livestreaming, rich data exchange, crowd commentary and curation, and matchmaking of various kinds. So, Sara's scenario is a focused fast-forward of all these technologies and techniques toward a brighter future for human ability.

That's right: part of the problem is necessary for the solution. But it's not the volatile part. Remember, technology *itself* is not causing *any* of the problems that we're experiencing with skill. We're the ones striking a deal with our increasingly intelligent tools: offer us techno-enhanced productivity, we'll sacrifice the expert-novice bond. Chapter 7 shows us that deal is *optional*. But to really supercharge our skill development—to levels yet unseen in the history of our species—we need a new, always-on, accessible, globe-scale infrastructure for ensuring healthy challenge, complexity, and connection. Humans alone aren't capable of something so complex. We need the best of human and nonhuman intelligences to make that vision manifest.

That means the future of skill might be a lot more futuristic than the one Sara lives in.

HOLD ON TO YOUR HATS

It's been a few decades since the internet really came online. A clear case of a general-purpose technology—unlike most, these are useful for most of us in many ways. Our economy, our work, our social lives, even our beliefs and preferences shift in big ways whenever we build them. Before the internet it would have been very hard to imagine the world after the internet. The same with

---

* A cloud-based platform that helps software developers store, manage, and collaborate with others on code.

steel, electricity, the steam engine, the internal combustion engine, the assembly line, the telegraph, and so on. And just a hot minute ago in 2023 we got open, free-to-use, chat-based generative AI—aka ChatGPT.[4] Another general-purpose technology, this time one that produces useful combinations of words, ideas, images, code, and so on. Many have called it "autocomplete for everything." Another moment it's hard to see beyond. So, we know that—if we're looking for a positive skills vision—there will be real possibilities in 2037 that would make a mockery of what I've presented. The skill upside could be far greater.

Let's pick just one example: prompting. Everywhere you look these days, you hear it: those who can craft just the right question for ChatGPT will get dramatically more useful output, and they'll race ahead. In the short run, this is clearly true: there's a huge difference between the response to "write an email to convince a pizza shop to stock my napkins" and "guide me to write a convincing email to sell napkins to a pizza shop, step by step. Teach me as if you had marketing guru Seth Godin's expertise and rely on the techniques and research in Matt Beane's *The Skill Code*." In many cases you'd be far better off if you could write prompt two. But it's already become clear that this is a temporary problem. By as soon as this year, we'll have commercially available systems that will automatically coach us toward more productive outcomes. In the napkins case? We might write the first prompt, and the system would reply, "I've got to ask you a couple of questions to make sure this gets you the sale. And by the way, do you want to get better at this by the time the email's done? That would only take a few extra minutes." No human in the loop. Just an AI-enabled engine that has two objectives: get the user the results they want and nudge them toward more skill. Sara might have something much closer to an active coach embedded in SkillNet—one she might even start to bond with, if it remembers their interactions and guides her over time.

But you should hold your hat even tighter than that. Maybe much tighter.

Let's start with computation. We're making steady progress to practical quantum computers—the very device that Sara was working on at her bench. Instead of representing the world in os and 1s, like a classical-computing binary unit, a qubit (short for quantum bit) can do that and hold both values at the same time. So instead of doing computations one at a time, quantum computers can do them all at once. Those performance figures I gave you are *today's* estimates as to what these devices should be able to do for us. And I understated the situation: in a few seconds, these systems could calculate certain things that a universe-sized conventional computer *never* could. Just for starters, this may supercharge simulation modeling for scientific discovery in chemistry, geophysics and climate, energy, and life sciences, and accelerate basic operations underlying machine learning (aka AI). It's hard to imagine domains that wouldn't be affected. The twist inside all this is that they've relied on AI to do their work for years—for example in modeling the heating properties of the ruby and diamond (no kidding) they grow as quantum computing substrates. So, the GPT revolution will serve as an uncertain but potent accelerant in all their work—they're going to be moving even faster. Are quantum computers ready now? No. Should you assume they won't be for twenty years? Fifteen? No.

So not only is AI hastening the arrival of this radically more powerful, general-purpose technology, but the technology itself will have profound implications for digital apprenticeship. What would SkillNet look like, what could it do for our skill, if it took advantage of functional quantum computers, combined with the GPT-style AI I mentioned above? You might start imagining how—hyperpersonalized, fine-grained guidance for each person on a moment-by-moment basis, modeling the huge complexity associated with an entire lifetime of task and skill choices, and so on—but good luck making solid predictions. One thing's for sure: the potential upside could make Sara's rosy story seem mediocre.

Head spinning a bit? Let it come to rest on fusion power: the promise of ridiculously safe, zero-emission, practically unlimited energy without any radioactive waste. Unlike quantum computing, the hope for fusion energy has been with us since the 1950s.[5]

Fast-forward to December 5, 2022. On this day, the fusion reactor at the US Department of Energy's National Ignition Facility produced more energy than it put in.[6] Basically, this was the moment in human history where the fusion fire—the heat and light thrown off by fused hydrogen atoms—was bigger than the match: in this case, 192 high-energy laser beams pointed at those atoms. Until that day, many very serious fusion scientists thought this milestone was thirty years away, just like it had been every year since the Cold War. Dennis Whyte, nuclear physicist at MIT and the director of the MIT Plasma Science and Fusion Center, thinks we're four years away from a commercially viable design,[7] and Microsoft just signed a deal to buy fusion energy from a startup called Helion Energy in five years.[8] And here, as with quantum computing, advanced AI—from Google's Deep Mind group as well as in academia—is helping scientists design the magnets and composites that go into these reactors, as well as modeling the behavior of the plasma (superheated gas that the magnets contain) where the fusion reaction takes place. The more the AI advances, the faster we run toward fusion.

If power were practically free, how would SkillNet run, where could we use it that we couldn't before, and to what positive effect? Again, we can imagine the implications—like better skill, for more people—but confidently claiming when and how these will play out is sheer folly. We just can't see clearly around a corner like this, let alone when several happen more or less at the same time.

I could go on. SpaceX has over four thousand satellites in orbit since they started launching them in May 2019.[9] These provide high-speed internet to about 1.5 million households in the rural

US alone. Their goal? Forty-two thousand satellites. So, we're all going to be more connected. SkillNet for more, faster. And the cost of a robot—the collection of sensors, plastics, metals, batteries, AI control software, and so on—is decreasing rapidly, their components are increasingly modular (swappable between robots), and instead of asking for tens or hundreds of thousands of dollars in cash, many firms are leasing their systems for each successful action they take, whether that be picking up a doggie treat or drilling holes in an aircraft fuselage. SkillNet might control—or let you supervise—a robotic practice buddy or two. On May 4, 2023, a paper published in *Nature*, one of the top two scientific journals on the planet, showed we can create video from brain waves. Not just any video, but video that's a very high-fidelity representation of what a rat was *actually seeing* at the time.[10] SkillNet could record what you were seeing without a bulky AR headset. Obviously, all of this is—at best—barely hitting the commercial market. But are we confident that it won't be widely available in the next twenty years? How about fifteen?

Any one of these technologies could allow for profound reconfiguration of a huge swath of the working world, including the challenge, complexity, and connection at the heart of skill development. Lots of very smart, very driven folks are working on all of them, simultaneously, and AI is allowing them to race even further, faster. We really are sitting on the nose cone of a rocket, pointed into the great beyond, and the boosters are already lit. We're headed somewhere, fast. But . . .

We may not want to get there.

THE SPECTER OF SKILL INEQUALITY

The sociologist in me doesn't operate on hope, positive exceptions, or possibilities. It sees social forces at work. Situations, practices, tools, institutions, and cultures that make certain outcomes more likely for anyone who gets involved. Deprive someone of resources like money and, on average, they start to behave and think like a poor person. Put someone in a social network with a certain set of political beliefs and, on average, they'll adopt them. Give us technology that allows us to get rapid productivity gains if we reduce novice involvement in the work? On average, we'll do it. From this point of view, the "safe" prediction from all the research I'm aware of—mine and others'—is that we will continue to weaken the expert-novice bond. We will degrade healthy challenge, complexity, and connection in our work, and the rare few who find shadow learning practices or who are lucky enough to avoid these traps will race ahead with far more skill than the rest of us.

We worry about income and wealth inequality these days. Serious problems. But right now, we are also racing down a road toward skill inequality, and the sociologist in me doesn't see any forces arising to change that on a mass scale.

We do not want to live in that future. First off, individuals who hit a wall on skill development will hit a wall on their careers, their income, and their quality of life. For most surgeons, this might mean getting blocked from top-tier hospitals, limits to income, and the stress of being behind the times—while a few race ahead to far more prestige, more miraculous patient "saves," and dramatically higher income. But skill inequality goes way deeper and darker than it will in high-status, highly paid professions. After spending three years interviewing hundreds of warehouse workers with my team, I can tell you firsthand that the aphorism attributed to William Gibson ("the future is already here—it's just not evenly distributed") is just as applicable here as in robotic surgery: *this* darker future is *also* already here, and it's heavily concentrated in low-wage, entry-level, repetitive work. These folks are often temporary workers. No benefits, no job security. Barely any training, practically zero mentorship. And warehousing corporations invest massive resources to aggressively *deskill* the jobs these folks occupy. Industrial engineers walk the floors, doing detailed time-motion studies to figure out how they could improve productivity. For a warehouse? That's how many items the building can process in a day, times a "defect" rate—or the percentage of units out of a hundred that don't get damaged, badly labeled, stolen, and so on. And what's the best way to increase throughput times quality? Reduce "skilled touches." Those industrial engineers know that every time a human has to deal with an item, there's a chance for an error. And that the more skill it takes to handle that item, the greater the chance of the error is. So they are continually redesigning the work to *extract* skill requirements from the job and quantify the output—not just reduce the number of times a human has to interact with the product. It's only one more step to the stark conclusion: the longer that a worker stays in jobs like this, the *less* skill they can expect to have over time. Their skill *degrades*.

That's degrad*ing*, too. A lot of folks, according to one worker, get to a place where they "are content with just doing the grunt work. I mean because a lot of these pick and pack places—it's like high school, do you know what I mean? You'd rather just stay in your lane in the palletizing and don't even get involved with the people up there [in other areas]." So long, healthy challenge and complexity. So long to healthy connection, too. Said another one: "Honestly, I can't [tell you about what my coworkers are like] because I don't talk to anybody there. We're trying to go so fast to make our numbers." And this last worker tells us the nasty conclusion—the longer you stay in a job like *that*, the less likely you are to look for something better: "there's a lot of warehouse jobs that you see people after being there for a while, and I just can tell they're drained, tired all the time, and just fed up of it but [they] don't really know anything else." Here and in many comparable places throughout the economy, we really are destroying human potential on a mass scale in the name of techno-productivity. Sita, and the rare few like her that my team and I found in warehouses all around the US, prove that we can build rich, valuable skill just about anywhere. Deskilling, degrading work is always optional. On top of that, Sita's, Inés's, and Gerardo's innovations show us that favoring skills over pure productivity isn't an act of charity or empathy alone. Insisting on skill development and productivity offers huge competitive business advantages, too—and opportunity costs if we stick with the skill-sacrificing status quo.

Sara's future—a world where the skill code is healthy and vibrant—will not write itself. Without a focused, massive investment, we're going to get more of the skills future I saw unfolding for most workers in warehouses. To pull this off—to stop the dark sociological skills prediction from coming true—we must build a new, global, AI-enabled infrastructure to strengthen these foundations of skill instead of undermining them. On that score, we need to take the very technologies we're concerned about—robotics, AI, cameras, the internet, mobile devices, and now large language models like ChatGPT—and use them to build the infrastructure for skill we need in the twenty-first century. And those with power in organizations need to weave this new infrastructure into all the tactics and orientations laid out in chapter 7—so they're more powerful than they would be otherwise. Sara knows: this is a future that brings humanity and technology into an even tighter dance where challenge, complexity, and connection thrive.

THE FUTURE OF SKILL IS CHIMERIC

In this new world, we would have a network of human experts, novices, and AI, focused on building human and AI capability right in the middle of work. As you saw in Sara's case, this goes way beyond AI-assisted matches between experts and novices who happen not to work in the same physical space or organization. This is literally a new fabric for the expert-novice connection—where simply by engaging with it, both humans and AI learn faster than they could on their own, enhancing human relationships and our sense of fulfillment along the way. A lot of the tools to enable this are already on the table: human-computer interaction researchers like Kurt Vanlehn and Michelene Chi at the University of Arizona have shown us interactive, automated systems that provide powerful assistance and even collaborative glue as learners seek skill.[11] Sometimes these help us build skill more than a human tutor would—a bounded but real solution to Bloom's "two sigma" problem. Generative AI offers significant opportunities to enrich and deepen this human-technology partnership, and our collective skill along with it.

We've started calling systems like these chimera. This was originally the name for an ancient Greek creature with a lion's head, a goat's body, and a serpent for a tail. A blend of different entities. A system is chimeric when it is neither human nor technological—one that allows us to take full advantage of both in ways that do better than either humans or AI could do alone. An early, clean example of this is in the world of chess. For centuries, humans were best at the game, competing and examining the game with fearsome intensity to advance the state of play. Then, in 1985, computer scientists at Carnegie Mellon started to develop a chess program they called "Chip Test."[12] But you probably know it by the name that IBM gave it after they took on the project in 1989: Deep Blue. In 1997, it won an exhibition match against Garry Kasparov, the great chess grandmaster. That was it, apparently: computers were best at chess. But it didn't last. Soon the best chess players were chimera—a human partnering with an AI won against a human alone or an AI alone. The AI could propose a complex tree of moves that had a high probability of success, given the lay of the board. But the human was best at intuiting play styles and taking considered risks. Ultimately AI rose to the top again, but chess isn't a complex problem compared to real life. When the board, the rules, and the number of players are shifting in unpredictable ways, chimera will have real staying power.

Some companies are using chimeric systems to help people become more effective in their jobs—like maintaining gas turbines, laying out computer chip designs, operating on cancerous tumors, and even harvesting crops. When designed carefully and deployed well, chimeric solutions scaffold the human to more productivity than either human or technology could achieve alone: subtle, early preventative maintenance that keeps a turbine spinning for less cost, ingenious chip layouts that save power, being *sure* you've gotten all the cancer in an operation, and doing far less damage to a crop as you navigate a combine with hyperhuman precision. But as you now know, today's chimera almost never develop that human's skill in the process. They don't promote healthy challenge, foster healthy complexity, or facilitate healthy connections between humans. In the short run, they give us great productivity; chimeras can sort tomatoes or trade securities like a fiend. But then the humans in that loop forget how to do these things and there is no chimeric skill-building system in place to redirect, utilize, and enhance that person's intelligence and capability. We don't have a digital apprenticeship to replace the analog one we're losing. To save human ability in an age of intelligent machines, we've got to build one. Starting *right now*.

Let's step away from that black mirror. For most of us, it's not here yet. And the great news is that Gibson is right in both directions: the technologies and systems evident in Sara's 2037 story are all in use today. They're just not evenly distributed.

THE BUILDING BLOCKS FOR A DIGITAL APPRENTICESHIP

The technical backbone for Sara's future is here in two forms: more integrated and closed systems and more discrete and open ones. The first are more organized but rigid, while the others are vibrant but chaotic. On the integrated side, we have corporate learning systems and online learning platforms like Khan Academy and Code.org. These can gather data on people's work assignments—when they're completed, time taken, and error rates on quizzes, for example—and allow administrators to enter rules, roles, tasks, credentials, and other guidelines. These are the building blocks for discrete learning: courses, micro-courses, career paths, and so on. These are, in turn, building blocks for longer-term experiences for focused skill development: A skills boot camp in coding for noncoders at a bank. A project management intensive for software engineers. A half-year reskilling program in critical care for nurses. Organizations often mandate how novices should progress, but it's *becoming* more open: people can browse around and discover their own way forward—through a combination of introductory content, new insight into their skills and potential direction, and talent marketplaces like Gloat that help managers, experts, and novices to democratize access to that next great work assignment to boost skills, results, and careers.

Integrated systems like these still have an overwhelming bias toward declarative knowledge—the kind of book learning that gets you a ticket to the ball game, not a position on the field. As you know by now, we build most of our valuable skill *after* we get that kind of content, and we usually get way too *much* of it, too early—it can really hinder solid skill because it deprives us of the struggle, implicit learning, and mentor-guided task performance that are core to healthy challenge, complexity, and connection. But there's real progress here: talent marketplaces and skills boot camps are much more focused on scaffolding people through the collaborative work experiences so that they end up with skill in the process. For example, at Code.org—an organization dedicated to getting computer science into K–12 education—after one or two years of more self-guided, learn-to-click-and-drag style material, many learning interactions play out in small groups trying to build software that solves increasingly challenging, real-world problems. On the corporate side, MentorCliq connects a company's experts with its novices for longer-term mentorships, sometimes integrated with their work. By connecting people on real work and giving them a chance to struggle and support one another, integrated systems can foster human connection in the process, too. Finally, many aspects of these systems now make finer-grained predictions and recommendations about useful content, career, job, and task options, and the quality of potential expert-novice matches in certain cases. And with GPT-style AI on board, this automated guidance will start coming through quite realistic voice- and text-based chats. It's already in place in Khan Academy's "Khanmigo" capability, which Sal Khan demonstrated on the TED stage in 2023—a system that coaches students to write fiction or do math, according to some of the best available research on what good coaching looks like.[13] This means the coaching is coming from the system directly—no human in the loop. And it can guide teachers to make the best use of their talents, too. Does this kind of capability reflect the skill code, in full? Not yet. Healthy connection between humans is absent, for example. But it's definitely headed in the right direction.

The other half of the set of building blocks we need for a digital apprenticeship is a buzzing, global ecosystem of more discrete and open technology. Even right now, we could put this all together to get breathtaking new insights about human capability and skill development, because the components are gathering and representing expert and novice behavior in new ways. What was once reserved for professional athletes and their millionaire coaches will now be available for the masses. On the platform side, think YouTube. On the data creation side, think cameras and keyboards. Platforms allow any internet-connected individual to create, share, consume, and interact around content in some form. YouTube alone may well be the single biggest skills-enhancing innovation since the printing press—how many times in the last month or two have you gone there for a quick how-to video, scanned the comments, then gone and solved a problem you couldn't before? I showed you that this is a critical part of how the best robotic surgeons in the world are learning now. The broader point here is that this is true for billions of us on many, many topics, and these are often focused on more procedural knowledge—tasks that are hard to describe precisely in language. Threaded, text-and-file based platforms like Stack Overflow offer complementary help—you can go there, post your problem, and an expert can give you pointers in minutes. You'll chip in on other folks' problems when you can, too, and everyone rates the helpfulness of various responses, so the helpful stuff becomes easier to find.

We don't much think about the data creation side: devices that convert real-world phenomena into digital information. The basic ingredients are sensors like cameras, microphones, antennas, scales, and accelerometers (a little gyroscope that can sense movement). These are rapidly falling in cost, so we build them into all kinds of things, including the tools we use to get work done. Two of these are remarkably familiar: keyboards and mice. Our input actions make these create data that computers can read and act on. Why does sensor data matter for skill? Experts and novices need rich, direct data on actual work activity—practice included—to decide on goals, direct practice and reflection, and guide their collaborative work. This kind of technology allows us to expand beyond the confines of our own sensors—eyes, ears, skin, tongues, noses—to get new, useful insight that can inform healthy challenge, complexity, and connection. How, exactly, is a pianist carrying too much stress as she plays? When, exactly, does a student drift off into multitasking and doomscrolling as they try to write? What is a therapist doing, precisely, as they fail to diagnose symptoms of depression? Cheaper, more diverse sensors give us a way to find out. In fact, part of what got me to drop a perfectly serviceable consulting career was discovering the "sociometric badges" being tested at Alex "Sandy" Pentland's lab at MIT.[14] You wore these small devices around your neck on a lanyard, and each had five sensors on board, capturing all kinds of data about interpersonal interaction between those who wore them. They could tell you—in real time—if you were talking too much or taking turns well in a conversation, who you spent the most time with, and how much you fidgeted as you spoke. Sandy and his students used this data to make shockingly accurate predictions about all kinds of important outcomes, from speed dating to startup pitches to group decision making. Expert-novice collaboration for skill could easily have been one of them.

There are massive problems with these technologies, of course. The main one is we're drinking from a fire hose of new data without a way of making sense of it. On the platform side, finding quality content is hard: the shadow learning surgeons I've studied spent an average of about twenty hours to find a high-quality video clip on YouTube that served their learning needs. The average resident didn't have that time. Only someone truly obsessed—who is willing to sacrifice those ten hours in sleep, time with a loved one or a patient—will find and learn from it. Novices across many occupations will settle on the first plausible content they find, which might steer them wrong, or at least not help. And platforms like these don't do much at all to foster healthy connection—good luck building a warm bond of trust and respect with Axlotl113 in the comments section on a video or in a code repo. On the data creation side, cheap sensors mean a glut of digitized information about how experts and novices work, and ironically that can decrease learning because nobody's quite sure what to do with it. Every warehousing company I studied had cameras in every building, for example. Did they examine that data to uncover and foster particularly effective or skillful work practices? No. The only time they looked at it was *after* an accident, altercation, or theft. Skill wasn't even on managers' minds—they were focused on ensuring reliable, safe operations. Beyond this, cheap, ubiquitous sensors raise all kinds of privacy and other ethical concerns—

remember the entire argument about surveillance and shadow learning in the previous chapter? We have to avoid the temptation to capture everything, lest we drive beneficial innovation into the darkness.

When it comes to the skill code, there are promising developments on both the platform and data creation sides of the equation. I'm a technology entrepreneur, not just an academic, so for over three years I've been hard at work building something in this territory with my colleague Juho Kim—a recognized expert in human-computer interaction for learning at the Korea Advanced Institute of Science & Technology. We call this first module Surch.[15]

Picture Beth—the shadow learning resident in chapter 1—sitting down at her computer at 2:19 in the morning. Her goal is to find a video clip of an anastomosis in an obese patient: that's what she's got to deal with in a few days. This is the part of a robotic prostatectomy where the prostate itself has been removed, and the bladder is disconnected from the urethra. The surgeon's job is to tie the bladder neck back to the urethra so the patient can go to the bathroom again: a leaky anastomosis is no joke. Beth built her skill without our technology, so she would have spent about ten hours looking for the right clip. Most videos are of healthy, normal-weight (that is to say, pretty unusual) patients, and she knows that doing this suturing job can be much harder if there's a lot of fatty tissue in the way. So, she searches. And searches. And searches.

The residents who have used our system in real clinical preparation find their clip—and the anastomosis within it—in a matter of seconds. And they can jump straight to the anastomosis with another click. The whole process takes less than a minute, which is about what most surgeons can afford to devote to this search problem. For video to be useful to their skill development, they need to get high-quality, on-target content in a hallway or a subway with a moment's notice. That's what we deliver. But we go way beyond this: across nine of the top teaching hospitals in the

US, residents don't just go find what they need—experts can give them assignments to do so. Someone like Kristen, a few years into her residency, might find an assignment to watch three videos, then send in a few comments contrasting how those surgeons approached the anastomosis. Then Doug, Kristen's attending, would review those answers and offer feedback. Doug gets a great new stream of information about Kristen's competence: What is she noticing? Is she drawing out the right detail? Highlighting potential issues correctly? He knows much better how much he can trust her surgical judgment. And Kristen gets a new stream of feedback and visibility in her work with him. Their connection gets enhanced, just as she gets new ways to engage with challenge and complexity.

This is all facilitated through a chimera: humans teaching an AI to teach humans to teach an AI to . . . you get the picture. We've enrolled a growing group of medical residents and top-notch surgeons to use the system for expert-novice learning interactions, and that produced training data: each time someone labeled where the phases in a procedure started or ended, for example. We've used their clicks and views to train an AI to classify and parse these videos in comparable ways. In the lingo of researchers focused on procedural knowledge, we're autogenerating a "semantic map" of each video—in his previous research, Juho called this "learner-sourcing."[16] This is like having an index for a book—finding what you want is a lot faster. We also have modules that allow for vicarious, collaborative connections between users, so they can share clips, tips, and comments. By the time this book goes to press, Juho and I hope to have the full suite out there, including a set of quality filters, and threaded, rated discussion among users—facilitating healthy challenge, complexity, and connection for experts and novice surgeons around the globe.

When we build chimeric platforms like this, we have the potential to not only salvage our skill development at work, but also rewrite the skill code so it's more powerful than ever. Juho and I have precisely this vision for our platform: especially if no-body else tries, we'll push to turn it into version 1.0 of a digital apprenticeship infrastructure for the planet. We'll offer tools that allow users to capture, study, and share any form of procedural knowledge—supported by AI and a global community of experts and novices, people could efficiently and collaboratively learn how to shuck oysters, remove tree stumps, change the oil in their cars, and perform countless other tasks. Of course, we'll be grateful and excited if our system makes a difference just for professionals try-ing to learn to use various medical devices. But the world needs healthy skill development now more than ever, and we aim to do everything we can to create an open and accessible infrastructure that will allow all of us to share in the world Sara lives in.

We need your help.

OUR CHOICES, OUR SKILL, OUR FUTURE

People, relationships, and choices sit at the core of this book, not technology. However wondrous and utterly necessary a chime-ric future for skill may seem, the only way it will come to pass is through our work, our relationships, and our choices. In the every-day insistence on excellence that animates the collaborative bond between experts and novices. In the suffering and waste created as we weaken that bond, seeking technologically enabled productivity. In the ingenuity and grit in the shadow learning that produces skill in spite of those barriers. These leave clues to each next healthy step in the journey, and we need to pay fierce attention to them if we want to forge a brighter tomorrow. None of this happens unless many of us take up the cause.

However much or little power you feel you have, you have a critical role in ushering in this future. If you're a novice at some-thing, we need you to protect the healthy challenge, complexity, and connection you need to build skill and get ahead. You'll be helping more than just yourself by making change as you pass through your social world, not least through the example you set for other novices nearby. If you're the expert at something, we need you to amplify and enrich the skills journey for the novices around you. You'll prove through example that there's a new ceiling out there for how well experts can foster skill development while also deepening human relationships. If you're a manager, responsible not only for people but for an organization and its technology, we need you to insist that productivity and human capital development are not at odds—and to give us specific, useful ways of getting more of both by blending them together. If you're an entrepreneur, building and selling the intelligent technologies of tomorrow, you have a huge opportunity and obligation to show the world that there's money *and* human welfare to be made with systems that make it *harder* for organizations to get productivity *without* developing skills at the same time. And if you're a policymaker, you can also distinguish yourself—and improve our collective lot—by investing public funds. One key role of government is to correct what economists call "negative externalities"—when our behavior creates trouble that we don't have to deal with immediately. The threat in this book is like pollution in that sense—firms get their short-run productivity boost, but don't feel the pain of robbing the next generation of its skill. Last year the US Department of Education spent $639 billion. How much should it spend next year to address the externality in this book? Each of us has agency and privileged access to a unique part of the skills opportunity we face, so each of us has a role in the discovery, development, and deployment of the skill code in the months and years ahead.

There will always be a dark side to the intelligent technologies we are creating, with unintended consequences that keep us up at night. But if we breathe new life into the skill code—and safeguard the meta-superpower that has gotten us this far—we will have all we need to adapt to whatever grows from the seeds of change we have already sown. Our challenge and opportunity: learn with intelligent machines so that we can show future generations how to do the same. We must protect healthy challenge, complexity, and connection when we can. We must learn from shadow learners, too. And we need to draw all this together to build and inhabit a new infrastructure for the expert-novice bond to equip the next generation. This is how we strengthen humanity's sacred path to skill and adaptability. In that world, we will continue to see one, do one, and teach one—just in a way that matches with this new world of work we're creating.

All those years ago, with my chin on that splintery fence post, I was transfixed as a master tinsmith guided a novice to properly hammer out a candleholder. I learned something about how they worked together, and how that rich, very human partnership built skill. That experience lit a flame inside me, and I've dedicated my career to understanding and improving it. But all of us know something about this process—about the skill code at the heart of this book—so all of us can do something to protect and enhance it for the road ahead. If this book lit a flame for you, take up its tools and get to work. We—and our skill—need your help now, more than ever.

GRATITUDE

T hank you for reading this book, but now, this section: everyone here lent essential help in making this book a reality, and your attention helps me honor them properly.

Without my wife, Kristen Kolakowski, this book would not be in your hands. For over five years, she provided a nourishing mix of insight, inspiration, and wonder that convinced me this book could be of service to many people. I've never had someone believe in me so unconditionally yet push me so effectively to be better than I was yesterday. This book is dedicated to you, Kristen. Our relationship is my life's greatest achievement, and my ability to be a better partner to you is my most treasured skill. I love you.

In 2009, Adam Grant agreed—based on a pretty thin connection—to review my application essays for PhD programs. His encouragement meant the world. He later made the connection that led to my TED Talk, advised me not to write a book, but then promptly connected me to a world-class agent when I said I'd written a proposal anyway. Adam, your persistent, creative, and generous help made this book possible. I will pay it forward.

I could not have asked for better book-writing partners than my agent, Jim Levine, and my editor, Hollis Heimbouch. You had the insight that unlocked a superb proposal, Jim, and from the first conversation you arranged with Hollis, it was obvious the three of us were singing off the same sheet of unwritten music. Hollis, you brought far more of your expertise and care to this manuscript than you had to, and your guidance was elegant and bold. Working with you both has been a deep education, a true privilege, and great fun. Thank you.

I must thank a few more. Andy McAfee, you selflessly provided critical activation energy, warm connections, and persistent support. Grace Rubenstein, you offered truly breathtaking editorial help—a master class, plain and simple. Brandon Lepine, you went above and beyond in helping me digest a hundred years of social science across seven disciplines. And to the hundreds of people who allowed me access to your everyday work and spoke openly about it—you are the real heroes here, if there are any. May the world learn from your example, and may we all build the kind of future you were struggling toward.

NOTES

CHAPTER ONE: THE SKILL CODE

1. Willeke Wendrich, *Archaeology and Apprenticeship: Body Knowledge, Identity, and Communities of Practice* (Tucson: University of Arizona Press, 2013).
2. P. Gärdenfors and A. Högberg, "The Archaeology of Teaching and the Evolution of Homo docens," *Current Anthropology* 58, no. 2 (2017): 188–208, https://doi.org/10.1086/691178; M. Lombard and M. N. Haidle, "Thinking a Bow-and-Arrow Set: Cognitive Implications of Middle Stone Age Bow and Stone-Tipped Arrow Technology," *Cambridge Archaeological Journal* 22, no. 2 (2012): 237–264, https://doi.org/10.1017/S095977431200025X; T. J. H. Morgan, N. T. Uomini, L. E. Rendell, L. Chouinard-Thuly, S. E. Street, H. M. Lewis, C. P. Cross, C. Evans, R. Kearney, I. de la Torre, A. Whiten, and K. N. Laland, "Experimental Evidence for the Co-evolution of Hominin Tool-Making Teaching and Language," *Nature Communications* 6, no. 1 (2015): 6029, https://doi.org/10.1038/ncomms7029.
3. L. Pray, "Discovery of DNA Structure and Function: Watson and Crick," *Nature Education* 1, no. 1 (2008): 100.
4. D. Acemoglu and P. Restrepo, "Robots and Jobs: Evidence from US Labor Markets," Working Paper 23285, National Bureau of Economic Research, 2017, https://doi.org/10.3386/w23285; J. Chung and Y. S.

Lee, "The Evolving Impact of Robots on Jobs," *ILR Review* 76, no. 2 (2023): 290–319, https://doi.org/10.1177/00197939221137822.

5. Katja Ridderbusch, "Robotically Assisted Surgery: 'The Wild West of Surgical Training,'" *U.S. News & World Report*, December 13, 2019, https://www.usnews.com/news/healthcare -of-tomorrow/articles/2019-12-13/training-for-robotically-assisted -surgery-evolves; Matt Simon, "Med Students Are Getting Terrible Training in Robotic Surgery," *Wired*, March 15, 2018, https://www .wired.com/story/med-students-are-getting-terrible-training-in -robotic-surgery/.

6. Matt Beane, "Robotic Surgery Turns Surgical Trainees into Spectators," *IEEE Spectrum*, July 5, 2022, https://spectrum.ieee .org/robotic-surgery#toggle-gdpr.

7. V. Patel, "Forgotten Generation: Junior Lawyers Share Their Struggles with Lockdown," Law.com International, November 17, 2020, https://www.law.com/international -edition/2020/11/17/forgotten-generation-junior-lawyers-share-their -struggles-with-lockdown/.

8. S. Brayne, "Big Data Surveillance: The Case of Policing," *American Sociological Review* 82, no. 5 (2017): 977–1008, https://doi.org/10 .1177/0003122417725865.

9. C. Anthony, "When Knowledge Work and Analytical Technologies Collide: The Practices and Consequences of Black Boxing Algorithmic Technologies," *Administrative Science Quarterly* 66, no. 4 (2021): 1173–1212, https://doi.org/10.1177/00018392211016755.

10. "2.1 Million Manufacturing Jobs Could Go Unfilled by 2030," National Association of Manufacturers, May 4, 2021, https://www .nam.org/2-1-million-manufacturing-jobs-could-go-unfilled-by-2030 -13743/?stream=workforce.

11. "C-Suite Outlook 2023: Challenges and Priorities for CEOs," Conference Board, January 12, 2023, https://www.conference-board .org/podcasts/ceo-perspectives/C-Suite-Outlook-2023-Challenges -and-Priorities-for-CEOs.

12. J. Schwartz et al., "Beyond Reskilling," Deloitte Insights, 2020, https://www2.deloitte.com/us/en/insights/focus/human-capital -trends/2020/reskilling-the-workforce-to-be-resilient.html.

13. *Workplace Learning & Development Report 2018*, LinkedIn Learning, https://learning.linkedin.com/resources/workplace-learning-report -2018?src=li-scin&veh=7010d000001BicLAASv2&cid=7010d00000 1BicLAAS&bf=1.

14. *2022 State of the Industry*, Association for Talent Development, retrieved August 30, 2023, from https://www.td.org/state-of-the -industry/2022-state-of-the-industry.

15. R. K. Merton, "Social Structure and Anomie," *American Sociological Review* 3, no. 5 (1938): 672–82, https://doi.org/10.2307/2084686.

CHAPTER TWO: CHALLENGE

1. M. A. Gernsbacher et al., "Making Things Hard on Yourself, but in a Good Way: Creating Desirable Difficulties to Enhance Learning," in *Psychology and the Real World: Essays Illustrating Fundamental Contributions to Society*, 2nd ed. (New York: Worth, 2014), 59–68.

2. M. A. Guadagnoli and T. D. Lee, "Challenge Point: A Framework for Conceptualizing the Effects of Various Practice Conditions in Motor Learning," *Journal of Motor Behavior* 36, no. 2 (2004): 212–24, https://doi.org/10.3200/JMBR.36.2.212-224.

3. K. Akizuki and Y. Ohashi, "Measurement of Functional Task Difficulty during Motor Learning: What Level of Difficulty Corresponds to the Optimal Challenge Point?" *Human Movement Science* 43 (2015): 107–17, https://doi.org/10.1016/j.humov.2015.07 .007.

4. S. Said et al., "Validation of the Raw National Aeronautics and Space Administration Task Load Index (NASA-TLX) Questionnaire to Assess Perceived Workload in Patient Monitoring Tasks: Pooled Analysis Study Using Mixed Models," *Journal of Medical Internet Research* 22, no. 9 (2020), https://doi.org/10.2196/19472.

5. K. Shabani, M. Khatib, and S. Ebadi, "Vygotsky's Zone of Proximal Development: Instructional Implications and Teachers' Professional Development," *English Language Teaching* 3, no. 4 (2010): 237–48.

6. B. S. Bloom, "The 2 Sigma Problem: The Search for Methods of Group Instruction as Effective as One-to-One Tutoring," *Educational Researcher* 13, no. 6 (1984): 4–16, https://doi.org/10 .3102/0013189X013006004.

7. D. Wood, J. S. Bruner, and G. Ross, "The Role of Tutoring in Problem Solving," *Journal of Child Psychology and Psychiatry* 17 (1976): 89–100.

8. J. Seely Brown, A. Collins, and P. Duguid, "Situated Cognition and the Culture of Learning," *Educational Researcher* 18, no. 1 (1989): 32–42.

9. Bloom, "The 2 Sigma Problem."

10. J. Van Maanen and P. K. Manning, "The Asshole," in *Policing: A View from the Street* (Santa Monica, CA: Goodyear, 1978), 307–28.

11. Jean Lave and Etienne Wenger, *Situated Learning: Legitimate Peripheral Participation* (Cambridge: Cambridge University Press, 1991), https://doi.org/10.1017/CBO9780511815355.

12. Karl E. Weick and Kathleen M. Sutcliffe, *Managing the Unexpected: Sustained Performance in a Complex World*, 3rd ed. (Hoboken, NJ: Wiley, 2015).

13. K. A. Ericsson, R. T. Krampe, and C. Tesch-Römer, "The Role of Deliberate Practice in the Acquisition of Expert Performance," *Psychological Review* 100, no. 3 (1993): 363–406, https://doi.org/10.1037/0033-295X.100.3.363.

14. A. H. Miller and C. L. Raison, "The Role of Inflammation in Depression: From Evolutionary Imperative to Modern Treatment Target," *Nature Reviews Immunology* 16, no. 1 (2016): 22–34, https://doi.org/10.1038/nri.2015.5.

15. K. L. Clark and B. Noudoost, "The Role of Prefrontal Catecholamines in Attention and Working Memory," *Frontiers in Neural Circuits* 8 (2013), https://doi.org/10.3389/fncir.2014.00033.

16. D. Cen, C. Gkoumas, and M. J. Gruber, "Anticipation of Novel Environments Enhances Memory for Incidental Information," *Learning & Memory* 28, no. 8 (2021): 254–59, https://doi.org/10.1101/lm.053392.121.

17. S. M. Hoscheidt et al., "Encoding Negative Events under Stress: High Subjective Arousal Is Related to Accurate Emotional Memory Despite Misinformation Exposure," *Neurobiology of Learning and Memory* 112 (2014): 237–47, https://doi.org/10.1016/j.nlm.2013.09.008.

18. J. Yang et al., "An Adversarial Training Framework for Mitigating Algorithmic Biases in Clinical Machine Learning," *Npj Digital Medicine* 6, no. 1 (2023): 1–10, https://doi.org/10.1038/s41746-023-00805-y.

19. A. Aggarwal, M. Mittal, and G. Battineni, "Generative Adversarial Network: An Overview of Theory and Applications," *International Journal of Information Management Data Insights* 1, no. 1 (2021): 100004, https://doi.org/10.1016/j.jjimei.2020.100004.

CHAPTER THREE: COMPLEXITY

1. J. Starkes, "A Multidimensional Approach to Skilled Perception and Performance in Sport," *Applied Cognitive Psychology* (1999).

2. John R. Anderson, *Language, Memory, and Thought* (Hillsdale, NJ: Erlbaum, 1976); Anderson, *The Architecture of Cognition* (Cambridge, MA: Harvard University Press, 1983).

3. T. D. Green and J. H. Flowers, "Implicit versus Explicit Learning Processes in a Probabilistic, Continuous Fine-Motor Catching Task," *Journal of Motor Behavior* 23 (1991): 293–300; Green and Flowers, "Comparison of Implicit and Explicit Learning Processes in a Probabilistic Task," *Perceptual and Motor Skills* 97 (2003): 299–314.

4. R. A. Magill, "Knowledge Is More than We Can Talk About: Implicit Learning in Motor Skill Acquisition," *Research Quarterly for Exercise and Sport* 69, no. 2 (1998): 104–10, https://doi.org/10 .1080/02701367.1998.10607676.

5. Albert Bandura and F. J. McDonald, "Influence of Social Reinforcement and the Behavior of Models in Shaping Children's Moral Judgment," *Journal of Abnormal and Social Psychology* 67, no. 3 (1963): 274–81, https://doi.org/10.1037/h0044714; Bandura, *Social Learning Theory* (Englewood Cliffs, NJ: Prentice-Hall, 1977).

6. A. M. Gentile, "A Working Model of Skill Acquisition with Application to Teaching," Quest Monograph 17 (1972): 3–23.

7. A. M. Gentile, "Skill Acquisition: Action, Movement, and Neuromotor Processes," in J. H. Carr et al., eds., *Movement Science: Foundations for Physical Therapy in Rehabilitation* (Rockville, MD: Aspen, 1987), 93–154.

8. P. M. Kruit, R. J. Oostdam, E. van den Berg, and J. A. Schuitema, "Effects of Explicit Instruction on the Acquisition of Students' Science Inquiry Skills in Grades 5 and 6 of Primary Education," *International Journal of Science Education* 40, no. 4 (2018): 41–41.

9. C. Goulet, C. Bard, and M. Fleury, "Expertise Differences in Preparing to Return a Tennis Serve: A Visual Information Processing Approach," *Journal of Sport and Exercise Psychology* 11 (1989): 382–98.

10. Magill, "Knowledge Is More than We Can Talk About: Implicit Learning in Motor Skill Acquisition."

11. Anders Ericsson and Robert Pool, *Peak: Secrets from the New Science of Expertise* (Boston: Houghton Mifflin Harcourt, 2016).

12. T. Schack and C. Frank, "Mental Representation and the Cognitive Architecture of Skilled Action," *Review of Philosophy and Psychology* 12 (2021): 527–46, https://doi.org/10.1007/s13164-020-00485-7.

13. D. A. Schön, "The Architectural Studio as an Exemplar of Education for Reflection-in-Action," *Journal of Architectural Education* 38

(1984):1, 2–9, https://doi.org/10.1080/10464883.1984.10758345; Schön, "From Technical Rationality to Reflection-in-Action," in *The Reflective Practitioner: How Professionals Think in Action* (New York: Basic Books, 1983), 21–69, 357–59.

14. E. R. Buch et al., "Consolidation of Human Skill Linked to Waking Hippocampo-Neocortical Replay," *Cell Reports* 35, no. 10 (2021): 109193, https://doi.org/10.1016/j.celrep.2021.109193.

15. R. S. W. Masters, "Knowledge Nerves and Know-how: The Role of Explicit versus Implicit Knowledge in the Breakdown of a Complex Motor Skill under Pressure," *British Journal of Psychology* 83 (1992): 343358; R. Masters and J. Maxwell, "The Theory of Reinvestment," *International Review of Sport and Exercise Psychology* 1, 2 (2008): 160–83; R. S. W. Masters, R. C. J. Polman, and N. V. Hammond, "Reinvestment: A Dimension of Personality Implicated in Skill Breakdown under Pressure," *Personality and Individual Differences* 14 (1993): 655666.

16. J. P. Maxwell, R. S. Masters, and F. F. Eves, "From Novice to No Know-how: A Longitudinal Study of Implicit Motor Learning," *Journal of Sports Sciences* 18, no. 2 (2000): 111–20, https://doi.org/10.1080/026404100365180, PMID: 10718567; J. P. Maxwell, R. S. Masters, and J. M. Poolton, "Performance Breakdown in Sport: The Roles of Reinvestment and Verbal Knowledge," *Research Quarterly for Exercise and Sport* 77 (2006): 271–76.

17. Kruit et al., "Effects of Explicit Instruction."

18. K. Jordan, R. Zajac, D. Bernstein, C. Joshi, and M. Garry, "Trivially Informative Semantic Context Inflates People's Confidence They Can Perform a Highly Complex Skill," *Royal Society Open Science* 9 (2022): 211977, https://doi.org/10.1098/rsos.211977.

19. Magill, "Knowledge Is More than We Can Talk About: Implicit Learning in Motor Skill Acquisition."

20. T. Drew, M. L.-H. Vo, and J. M. Wolfe, "The Invisible Gorilla Strikes Again: Sustained Inattentional Blindness in Expert Observers," *Psychological Science* 24, no. 9 (2013): 1848, https://doi.org/10.1177/0956797613479386.

21. Julian E. Orr, *Talking about Machines: An Ethnography of a Modern Job* (Ithaca, NY: Cornell University Press, 1996).

22. A. Nestor, J. M. Vettel, and M. J. Tarr, "Internal Representations for Face Detection: An Application of Noise-Based Image Classification to BOLD Responses," *Human Brain Mapping* 34 (2013): 3101–15, https://doi.org/10.1002/hbm.22128; M. Piana, M. Canfora, and

M. Riani, "Role of Noise in Image Processing by the Human Perceptive System," *Physical Review: E, Statistical Physics, Plasmas, Fluids, and Related Interdisciplinary Topics* 62 (1 Pt B) (2000): 1104–9, https://doi.org/10.1103/physreve.62.1104.

23. R. C. O'Reilly et al., "Recurrent Processing during Object Recognition," *Frontiers in Psychology* 4 (2013): 34845, https://doi.org/10.3389/fpsyg.2013.00124.

24. S. Thorat, G. Aldegheri, and T. C. Kietzmann, "Category-Orthogonal Object Features Guide Information Processing in Recurrent Neural Networks Trained for Object Categorization," *ArXiv* (2021): abs/2111.07898.

25. N. Srivastava, G. Hinton, I. Sutskever, and R. Salakhutdinov, "Dropout: A Simple Way to Prevent Neural Networks from Overfitting," *Journal of Machine Learning Research* 15 (2014): 1929–58.

CHAPTER FOUR: CONNECTION

1. R. M. Ryan and E. L. Deci, "Self-Determination Theory and the Facilitation of Intrinsic Motivation, Social Development, and Well-being," *American Psychologist* 55 (2000): 68–78.

2. E. L. Deci, A. H. Olafsen, and R. M. Ryan, "Self-Determination Theory in Work Organizations: The State of a Science," *Annual Review of Organizational Psychology and Organizational Behavior* 4, no. 1 (2017): 19–43, https://doi.org/10.1146/annurev-orgpsych-032516-113108.

3. J. Van Maanen, "The Smile Factory: Work at Disneyland," in P. J. Frost, L. F. Moore, M. R. Louis, C. C. Lundberg, and J. Martin, eds., *Reframing Organizational Culture* (Newbury Park, CA: Sage, 1991), 58–76.

4. A. Tintori, G. Ciancimino, R. Palomba, C. Clementi, and L. Cerbara, "The Impact of Socialisation on Children's Prosocial Behaviour: A Study on Primary School Students," *International Journal of Environmental Research and Public Health* 18, no. 22 (2021): 12017, https://doi.org/10.3390/ijerph182212017; H. Sadeghi Avval Shahr, S. Yazdani, and L. Afshar, "Professional Socialization: An Analytical Definition," *Journal of Medical Ethics and History of Medicine* (2019): 12, 17, https://doi.org/10.18502/jmehm.v12i17.2016.

5. Douglas A. Harper, *Working Knowledge: Skill and Community in a Small Shop* (Berkeley: University of California Press, 1992).

6. K. E. Kram, "Phases of the Mentor Relationship," *Academy of Management Journal* 26, no. 4 (1983): 608–25, https://doi.org/10.2307/255910.

7. Erik Erikson, *Childhood and Society* (New York: Norton, 1963); Erikson, *Identity, Youth, and Crisis* (New York: Norton, 1968).

8. R. M. Ryan and E. L. Deci, "Intrinsic and Extrinsic Motivation from a Self-Determination Theory Perspective: Definitions, Theory, Practices, and Future Directions," *Contemporary Educational Psychology* 61 (2020): 101860, https://doi.org/10.1016/j.cedpsych.2020.101860.

9. A. Martin and H. Marsh, "Academic Buoyancy: Towards an Understanding of Students' Everyday Academic Resilience," *Journal of School Psychology* 46 (2008): 53–83, https://doi.org/10.1016/j.jsp.2007.01.002.

10. A. E. Colbert, J. E. Bono, and R. K. Purvanova, "Flourishing via Workplace Relationships: Moving Beyond Instrumental Support," *Academy of Management Journal* 59 (2016): 1199–1223, https://doi.org/10.5465/amj.2014.0506.

11. D. M. Rousseau, S. B. Sitkin, R. S. Burt, and C. Camerer, "Not So Different after All: A Cross-Discipline View of Trust," *Academy of Management Review* 23, no. 3 (1998): 393–404.

12. Howard S. Becker, Everett C. Hughes, Blanche Geer, and Anselm L. Strauss, *Boys in White: Student Culture in Medical School* (Chicago: University of Chicago Press, 1961).

13. Michael Burawoy, *Manufacturing Consent: Changes in the Labor Process under Monopoly Capitalism* (Chicago: University of Chicago Press, 1979).

14. H. H. Brower et al., "A Closer Look at Trust Between Managers and Subordinates: Understanding the Effects of Both Trusting and Being Trusted on Subordinate Outcomes," *Journal of Management* (2008), https://doi.org/10.1177/0149206307312511.

15. J. R. Kogan, B. J. Hess, L. N. Conforti, and E. S. Holmboe, "What Drives Faculty Ratings of Residents' Clinical Skills? The Impact of Faculty's Own Clinical Skills," *Academic Medicine* 85 (10 Suppl) (2010): S25-8, https://doi.org/10.1097/ACM.0b013e318ied1aa3, PMID: 20881697.

16. L. Sheu, J. R. Kogan, and K. E. Hauer, "How Supervisor Experience Influences Trust, Supervision, and Trainee Learning: A Qualitative Study," *Academic Medicine* 92, no. 9 (2017): 1320–27, https://doi.org/10.1097/ACM.0000000000001560, PMID: 28079727.

17. K. E. Weick and K. H. Roberts, "Collective Mind in Organizations: Heedful Interrelating on Flight Decks," *Administrative Science Quarterly* (1993): 357–81.

18. H. Z. Gvirts and R. Perlmutter, "What Guides Us to Neurally and Behaviorally Align with Anyone Specific? A Neurobiological Model Based on fNIRS Hyperscanning Studies," *Neuroscientist* 26, no. 2 (2020): 108–16, https://doi.org/10.1177/1073858419861912.

19. Y. Pan, X. Cheng, Z. Zhang, X. Li, and Y. Hu, "Cooperation in Lovers: An fNIRS-Based Hyperscanning Study," *Human Brain Mapping* 38, no. 2 (2017): 831–41, https://doi.org/10.1002/hbm .23421, PMID: 27699945, PMCID: PMC6867051.

20. J. J. Teven and J. C. McCroskey, "The Relationship of Perceived Teacher Caring with Student Learning and Teacher Evaluation," *Communication Education* 46, no. 1 (1997): 1–9, https://doi.org/10 .1080/03634529709379069.

21. A. Edmondson, "Psychological Safety and Learning Behavior in Work Teams," *Administrative Science Quarterly* (1999), https://doi .org/10.2307/2666999; I. M. Nembhard and A. C. Edmondson, "Making It Safe: The Effects of Leader Inclusiveness and Professional Status on Psychological Safety and Improvement Efforts in Health Care Teams," *Journal of Organizational Behavior* 27, no. 7 (2006): 941–66, https://doi.org/10.1002/job.413; A. C. Edmondson, R. M. Bohmer, and G. P. Pisano, "Disrupted Routines: Team Learning and New Technology Implementation in Hospitals," *Administrative Science Quarterly* (2001), https://doi .org/10.2307/3094828.

22. M. C. Higgins and K. E. Kram, "Reconceptualizing Mentoring at Work: A Developmental Network Perspective," *Academy of Management Review* 26, no. 2 (2001): 264–88, https://doi.org/10 .2307/259122.

23. Edwin Hutchins, *Cognition in the Wild* (Cambridge, MA: MIT Press, 1995).

24. B. A. Bechky, "Gaffers, Gofers, and Grips: Role-Based Coordination in Temporary Organizations," *Organization Science* 17, no. 1 (2006): 3–21.

25. D. E. Bailey, P. M. Leonardi, and S. R. Barley, "The Lure of the Virtual," *Organization Science* 23, no. 5 (2012): 1485–1504.

26. N. Ducheneaut, "Socialization in an Open Source Software Community: A Socio-Technical Analysis," *Computer Supported Cooperative Work* 14, no. 4 (2005): 323–68, https://doi.org/10 .1007/s10606-005-9000-1.

27. Richard E. Ocejo, *Masters of Craft: Old Jobs in the New Urban Economy* (Princeton, NJ: Princeton University Press, 2017), https://doi.org/10.1515/9781400884865.

28. Anthony, "When Knowledge Work and Analytical Technologies Collide: The Practices and Consequences of Black Boxing Algorithmic Technologies."

29. B. Jordan, "Cosmopolitical Obstetrics: Some Insights from the Training of Traditional Midwives," *Social Science & Medicine* 28, no. 9 (1989): 925–37, discussion 937–44, https://doi.org/10.1016/0277-9536(89)90317-1.

30. M. A. Covaleski et al., "The Calculated and the Avowed: Techniques of Discipline and Struggles Over Identity in Big Six Public Accounting Firms," *Administrative Science Quarterly* 43, no. 2 (1998): 293–327, https://doi.org/10.2307/2393854.

31. M. Andrychowicz et al., "Learning to Learn by Gradient Descent by Gradient Descent," *ArXiv* (2016): /abs/1606.04474.

32. P. Christiano et al., "Deep Reinforcement Learning from Human Preferences," *ArXiv* (2017): /abs/1706.03741.

CHAPTER FIVE: THE THREAT

1. https://quoteinvestigator.com/2012/01/24/future-has-arrived/.

2. M. Beane, "Shadow Learning: Building Robotic Surgical Skill When Approved Means Fail," *Administrative Science Quarterly* (2018), https://doi.org/10.1177/0001839217751692.

3. N. Emanuel, E. Harrington, and A. Pallais, "The Power of Proximity to Coworkers: Training for Tomorrow or Productivity Today?" July 23, 2023, https://nataliaemanuel.github.io/ne_website/EHP_Power_of_Proximity.pdf.

4. J. J. Sandvik, R. E. Saouma, N. T. Seegert, and C. T. Stanton, "Workplace Knowledge Flows," *Quarterly Journal of Economics* 135, no. 3 (2020): 1635–80.

5. E. W. Felten, M. Raj, and R. Seamans, "How Will Language Modelers Like ChatGPT Affect Occupations and Industries?" (2023), https://ssrn.com/abstract=4375268 or http://dx.doi.org/10.2139/ssrn.4375268.

6. T. Eloundou, S. Manning, P. Mishkin, and D. Rock, "GPTs Are GPTs: An Early Look at the Labor Market Impact Potential of Large Language Models," *ArXiv* (2023): /abs/2303.10130.

7. "Accenture Study Finds U.S. Workers Under Pressure to Improve Skills but Need More Support from Employers," Accenture, November 16, 2011, https://newsroom.accenture.com/news/accenture-study-finds-us-workers-under-pressure-to-improve-skills-but-need-more-support-from-employers.htm.

8. P. Osterman, "How American Adults Obtain Work Skills: Results of a New National Survey," *ILR Review* 75, no. 3 (2022): 578–607, https://doi.org/10.1177/00197939211018191.

9. Brayne, "Big Data Surveillance: The Case of Policing," 977–1008.

10. B. Shestakofsky, "Working Algorithms: Software Automation and the Future of Work," *Work and Occupations* (2017), https://doi.org/10.1177/0730888417726119.

11. M. Beane and W. J. Orlikowski, "What Difference Does a Robot Make? The Material Enactment of Distributed Coordination," *Organization Science* 26, no. 6 (2015): 1553–73, https://doi.org/10.1287/orsc.2015.1004.

12. V. H. Murthy, "Our Epidemic of Loneliness and Isolation: The U.S. Surgeon General's Advisory on the Healing Effects of Social Cohesion and Community," Office of the Surgeon General, 2023.

CHAPTER SIX: LEARNING FROM THE SHADOWS

1. Nathan Zeldes, "Intrapreneurship and the Hewlett Packard Medal of Defiance," May 24, 2013, https://www.nathanzeldes.com/blog/2013/05/intrapreneurship-and-the-hewlett-packard-medal-of-defiance/.

2. Merton, "Social Structure and Anomie," 672–82.

3. Kai T. Erikson, *Wayward Puritans: A Study in the Sociology of Deviance* (New York: Wiley, 1966).

4. T. Schlich, "Surgery, Science and Modernity: Operating Rooms and Laboratories as Spaces of Control," *History of Science* 45, no. 3 (2007): 231–56.

5. F. Cartwright, "Joseph Lister," *Encyclopædia Britannica*, 2023, https://www.britannica.com/biography/Joseph-Lister-Baron-Lister-of-Lyme-Regis.

6. T. Schlich, "Farmer to Industrialist: Lister's Antisepsis and the Making of Modern Surgery in Germany," *Notes and Records of the Royal Society of London* 67, no. 3 (2013): 245–60.

7. Michael Worboys, *Spreading Germs: Disease Theories and Medical*

Practice in Britain, 1865–1900 (Cambridge: Cambridge University Press, 2000).

8. M. Worboys, "Joseph Lister and the Performance of Antiseptic Surgery," *Notes and Records of the Royal Society of London* 67, no. 3 (2013): 199–209, https://doi.org/10.1098/rsnr.2013.0028.

9. J. Lister, "On a New Method of Treating Compound Fracture, Abscess, etc.: With Observations on the Conditions of Suppuration," *Lancet* 89, no. 2272 (1867): 326–29.

10. A. Chodos and J. Ouellette, "December 1898: The Curies Discover Radium," American Physical Society, 2023, https://www.aps .org/publications/apsnews/200412/history.cfm.

11. Margaret Cheney, *Tesla: Man Out of Time* (New York: Touchstone Books, 2001).

12. J. Cunningham and N. Myhrvold, "Ferran Adria," 2023, *Encyclopædia Britannica*, https://www.britannica .com/biography/Ferran-Adria.

13. M. Beane, "Shadow Learning: Building Robotic Surgical Skill When Approved Means Fail," *Administrative Science Quarterly* 64, no. 1 (2019): 87–123, https://doi.org/10.1177/0001839217751692.

14. E. Holmboe, S. Ginsburg, and E. Bernabeo, "The Rotational Approach to Medical Education: Time to Confront Our Assumptions?" *Medical Education* 45 (2011): 69–80.

15. American College of Surgeons, Statement on Principles, April 12, 2016, https://www.facs.org/about-acs/statements/statements-on -principles/.

16. M. Beane and C. Anthony, "Inverted Apprenticeship: How Senior Occupational Members Develop Practical Expertise and Preserve Their Position When New Technologies Arrive," *Organization Science* (2023), https://doi.org/10.1287/orsc.2023.1688.

CHAPTER SEVEN: REWORKING THE SKILL CODE

1. Matt Buchanan, "Object of Interest: The PackBot," *New Yorker*, April 23, 2013, https://www.newyorker.com/tech/annals-of -technology/object-of-interest-the-packbot.

2. "iRobot to Create Revolutionary New Robot for DARPA," press release, iRobot Corporation, June 17, 2008, https://investor.irobot .com/news-releases/news-release-details/irobot-create-revolutionary -new-robot-darpa.

3. J. P. Kotter, "Leading Change: Why Transformation Efforts Fail," *Harvard Business Review* 73 (1995): 59–67.

4. Anthony, "When Knowledge Work and Analytical Technologies Collide: The Practices and Consequences of Black Boxing Algorithmic Technologies."

CHAPTER EIGHT: SKILL'S CHIMERIC FUTURE

1. Apple Vision Pro, 2023, Apple, https://www.apple.com/apple-vision -pro/.

2. Meta Quest 2, 2020, Meta, https://www.meta.com/gb/quest /products/quest-2/.

3. "How Google's Knowledge Graph Works—Knowledge Panel Help," Google, 2019, https://support.google .com/knowledgepanel/answer/9787176?hl=en; K. Marple, "Creating Enterprise Knowledge Graphs from Unstructured Data—Events," Microsoft, May 4, 2022, https://learn.microsoft.com/en-us/events /azure-cosmos-db-conf-2022/creating-enterprise-knowledge-graphs -from-unstructured-data.

4. Natalie, "ChatGPT—Release Notes," OpenAI, 2023, https://help .openai.com/en/articles/6825453-chatgpt-release-notes.

5. EUROfusion Consortium Research Institutions, "History of Fusion," June 30, 2023, https://euro-fusion.org/fusion/history-of -fusion/.

6. B. Bishop, "Lawrence Livermore National Laboratory Achieves Fusion Ignition," Lawrence Livermore National Laboratory, 2022, https://www.llnl.gov/news/lawrence-livermore-national-laboratory -achieves-fusion-ignition.

7. Lex Clips, "When Will Nuclear Fusion Power Plants Become Reality? Dennis Whyte and Lex Fridman," video, YouTube, 2023, https://www.youtube.com/watch?v=nbO9holQk6k.

8. J. Calma, "Microsoft Just Made a Huge, Far-from-Certain Bet on Nuclear Fusion," The Verge, May 10, 2023, https://www.theverge .com/2023/5/10/23717332/microsoft-nuclear-fusion-power-plant -helion-purchase-agreement.

9. Michael Kan, "SpaceX's Starlink Now Has Over 4,000 Satellites in Orbit," *PCMag*, May 4, 2023, https://www.pcmag.com/news/spacexs -starlink-now-has-over-4000-satellites-in-orbit.

10. S. Schneider, J. H. Lee, and M. W. Mathis, "Learnable Latent

Embeddings for Joint Behavioural and Neural Analysis," *Nature* 617 (2023): 360–68, https://doi.org/10.1038/s41586-023-06031-6.

11. K. Vanlehn, "The Relative Effectiveness of Human Tutoring, Intelligent Tutoring Systems, and Other Tutoring Systems," *Educational Psychologist* 46, no. 4 (2011): 197–221, https://doi.org/10 .1080/00461520.2011.611369; M. T. Chi and R. Wylie, "The ICAP Framework: Linking Cognitive Engagement to Active Learning Outcomes," *Educational Psychologist* 49, no. 4 (2014): 219–43.

12. Feng-Hsiung Hsu, *Behind Deep Blue: Building the Computer That Defeated the World Chess Champion* (Princeton, NJ: Princeton University Press, 2022).

13. Sal Khan, "How AI Could Save (Not Destroy) Education," TED Talks, 2023, https://www.ted.com/talks/sal_khan_how_ai_could_save_not _destroy_education?language=en.

14. S. Pentland, T. Kim, B. Waber, and D. Olguin-Olguin, "Sociometric Badges," MIT Media Laboratory, 2023, https://hd.media.mit .edu/badges/about.html.

15. J. Kim, D. Choi, N. Lee, M. Beane, and J. Kim, "2023 CHI Conference on Human Factors in Computing Systems," in *Proceedings of the 2023 CHI Conference on Human Factors in Computing Systems* (Hamburg: Association for Computing Machinery, 2023).

16. S. Weir, J. Kim, K. Z. Gajos, and R. C. Miller, "Learnersourcing Subgoal Labels for How-to Videos," in *Proceedings of the 18th ACM Conference on Computer Supported Cooperative Work & Social Computing* (Hamburg: Association for Computing Machinery, 2015), 405–16.

INDEX

ABOUT THE AUTHOR

M
ATT BEANE does field research on work involving robots and AI to uncover systematic positive exceptions that we can use across the broader world of work. His award-winning research has been published in top management journals such as *Administrative Science Quarterly* and *Harvard Business Review*, and he has spoken on the TED stage. He also took a two-year hiatus from his PhD at MIT's Sloan School of Management to help found and fund Humatics, a full-stack IoT startup. In 2012 he was selected as a Human-Robot Interaction Pioneer, and in 2021 was named to the Thinkers50 Radar list. Beane is an assistant professor in the Technology Management department at the University of California, Santa Barbara, and a Digital Fellow with Stanford's Digital Economy Lab and MIT's Initiative on the Digital Economy. When he's not studying intelligent technologies and learning, he enjoys playing guitar; his morning coffee ritual with his wife, Kristen; and reading science fiction—a lot of science fiction. He lives in Santa Barbara, California.